THE COMPLETE
CAT
BREED
BOOK

THE COMPLETE CAT BREED BOOK

Consultant Editor
DR. KIM DENNIS-BRYAN

LONDON, NEW YORK, MELBOURNE, MUNICH, AND DELHI

DORLING KINDERSLEY

Senior Editor Paula Regan
Project Art Editor Laura Roberts-Jensen
Additional Design Tannishtha Chakraborty, Amy Orsborne
Editorial Assistant Alexandra Beeden
Editors Lizzie Munsey, Steve Setford
Jacket Editor Manisha Majithia
Jacket Designer Laura Brim
Jacket Design Development Manager Sophia Tampakopoulos
DK Picture Library Claire Bowers, Claire Cordier, Emma Shepherd
Commissioned Photography Tracy Morgan
Database Rob Laidler, David Roberts
Senior Producer, Pre-Production Ben Marcus
Producer Gemma Sharpe
Managing Editor Esther Ripley
Managing Art Editor Karen Self
Publisher Laura Buller
Art Director Phil Ormerod
Associate Publishing Director Liz Wheeler
Publishing Director Jonathan Metcalf

Consultant Editor Kim Dennis-Bryan
Contributors Ann Baggaley, Jolyon Goddard, Wendy Horobin

DK INDIA

Managing Editor: Pakshalika Jayaprakash
Senior Editor: Sreshtha Bhattacharya
Editors: Antara Moitra, Nandini Gupta
Assistant Editor: Archana Ramachandran
Managing Art Editor: Romi Chakraborty
Senior Art Editor: Govind Mittal
Art Editors: Mahipal Singh, Amit Varma
Assistant Art Editors: Tanvi Sahu, Tanvi Nathyal
Design Consultant: Shefali Upadhyay
Picture Researcher: Sakshi Saluja
DTP Manager/CTS: Balwant Singh
DTP Designers: Mohammad Usman, Sachin Singh, Vishal Bhatia
Production Manager: Pankaj Sharma

First published in Great Britain in 2013 by Dorling Kindersley Limited
80 Strand, London WC2R 0RL

A Penguin Company

Copyright © 2013 Dorling Kindersley Limited

2 4 6 8 10 9 7 5 3 1

001 - 185340 - 05/13

Printed and bound in China by Leo Paper Products Ltd

Discover more at
www.dk.com

CONTENTS

1 INTRODUCTION TO CATS

INTRODUCTION TO CATS

WHAT IS A CAT?

The domestic cat is now the world's most popular pet, but cats were not always tame. The relationship between humans and cats began in the Near East about 10,000 years ago, when cats killed the rodents that ate grain stored in towns and villages. They were kept as pets in Egypt from about 2000 BCE, but the different breeds have only been created over the last hundred years or so.

Cats are fast-moving natural athletes

Evolution of the cat

The family history of the domestic cat goes way back in time, to long before the first human-like primates walked the Earth. All cats – from tigers, jaguars, and other big cats to smaller lynxes and ocelots – belong to the family of mammals called Felidae, which contains 41 living species. The first cat-like carnivores appeared around 35 million years ago. Fossil evidence suggests that modern felids arose in Asia about 11 million years ago. However, the big cats we know today, such as the lion, did not evolve until much later, between 4 and 2 million years ago, when a drier, warmer climate gave rise to open habitats and herds of soft-skinned grazing animals. The athletic build of big cats was ideal for catching such prey. Less agile types of cats, such as the sabretooths, gradually died out.

The most recent cats to evolve include the lynxes (USA and Europe), the bobcat (USA), the leopard cat (Southeast Asia), and the wildcats (Africa, Europe, and Asia). The domestic cat is descended from the African wildcat, and it is generally considered to be a wildcat subspecies.

Domestication

In the Near East, about 10,000 years ago, humans began growing cereal crops and storing grain for the first time. They found that rats and mice would get into their stores and eat the grain. However, the rodents themselves were eaten by small predators, such as the African wildcat. Soon a relationship between cats and humans developed: the cats had a ready supply of food in the rodents that

THE CAT FAMILY

■ **This diagram** shows the relationship between the domestic cat and some of the other members of the cat family – the Felidae – based on genetic evidence. The closer a cat is to the domestic cat on this diagram, the more similar their genetic make-up.

■ **All Felidae** are carnivores – they eat exclusively meat and could not survive on a plant-based diet.

■ **Though they vary** in size, most cats share some physical characteristics – they have lithe, muscular bodies, large eyes, and retractable claws, and most have tails that measure up to half their body length.

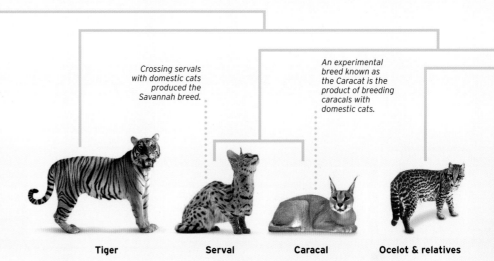

Crossing servals with domestic cats produced the Savannah breed.

An experimental breed known as the Caracat is the product of breeding caracals with domestic cats.

Tiger   **Serval**   **Caracal**   **Ocelot & relatives**

humans attracted, and the humans gained a much-appreciated form of pest control that lived alongside them in their towns and villages.

Wild species of cats are naturally wary of humans, but over time natural selection favoured those cats that were least scared of people and adaptable enough to change from being solitary hunters to living in close proximity to humans and other cats. By around 2000 BCE the cat had become fully domesticated and was living in the homes of the Ancient Egyptians as a much-loved pet that also kept rodents under control. From Egypt the domestic cat would eventually spread right around the world.

Cat breeds

In the late 19th century the breeding and showing of cats began in earnest, and cat enthusiasts became known as "cat fanciers". Cat registries were established to set breed standards and to store the genealogies of pedigree cats. Today, there are several international cat registries, and more than 100 different cat breeds, though not all registries recognize the same ones. Breeds are defined by characteristics such as body and head shape; coat colour and pattern; eye shape and colour; and temperament; as well as by unusual features such as hairlessness, short tails, and folded ears.

Pedigree cats have been selectively bred over many generations to perfect the desired characteristics of their breed. However, it is still possible for two cats in the same litter to be classed as different breeds, depending on which features they inherit from their parents.

WILD BEHAVIOUR
Domestic cats display many of the same instincts as their wild relatives. For example, they stretch frequently, to keep their muscles limber in case they need to sprint after prey or away from danger.

Early cat breeds were often "natural" breeds, typical of certain regions of the world. These include the Maine Coon (from the state of Maine, eastern USA) and the Turkish Van (from Turkey). Today, breeders understand how traits are inherited and use cats with novel characteristics to produce new breeds – for example, with curled ears. New breeds can also result from crossing domestic cats with wild relatives, such as the Bengal (part leopard cat) and Savannah (part serval). Most pet cats are randomly bred "moggies", without any defined breed.

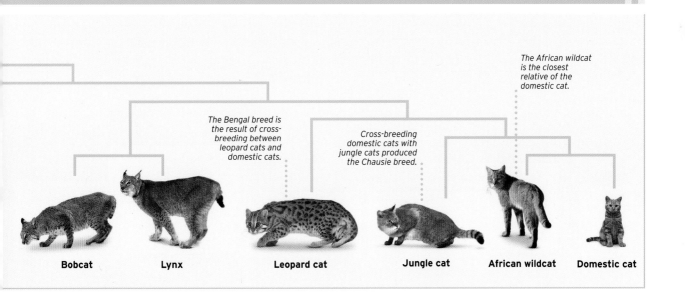

The Bengal breed is the result of cross-breeding between leopard cats and domestic cats.

Cross-breeding domestic cats with jungle cats produced the Chausie breed.

The African wildcat is the closest relative of the domestic cat.

Bobcat   **Lynx**   **Leopard cat**   **Jungle cat**   **African wildcat**   **Domestic cat**

The founder effect

Domestic cats spread around the world from Egypt, travelling with humans along trade routes on land and also aboard ships sailing to newly "discovered" lands, such as the Americas. These cats soon established isolated populations in new locations. If any of the "pioneer" cats in an area possessed an unusual trait, that characteristic stood a good chance of becoming common in future generations. In larger populations of mixed cats, these traits would usually disappear, especially if they caused disease or a disadvantage.

The genetic influence of these pioneering cats is known as the founder effect, and it explains why certain unusual traits still persist in some regions today. The best-known examples of the founder effect are the taillessness seen in the Manx cats of the Isle of Man and the polydactylism (a genetic mutation producing extra toes) that is common in cats along the East Coast of North America.

COAT LENGTH AND GENETICS
The length of a cat's coat is controlled by a gene – the most common form produces a short coat. This is dominant over the form that gives a long coat, so if a cat has a copy of each it will be shorthaired.

Cat genetics

Genes carry all the information necessary for life. They control not only the chemical processes in a cat's body, but also the information that dictates the cat's physical characteristics, such as eye colour and shape, coat colour, and coat length. Genes are found on structures called chromosomes, which are located in the nuclei of body cells. Domestic cats have 38 chromosomes – two sets of 19 corresponding pairs. One set of chromosomes is inherited from the father, and the other set from the mother. Because there are two sets of chromosomes, a cat has two copies of every gene (one from each parent), and some genes have variants that may produce different traits or characteristics.

If just one copy of a gene is needed for a trait to appear, that gene is called a "dominant" gene – for example, the gene for a tabby coat is dominant. If two copies of a gene are needed for

A CAT WITH MANY TOES
Cats with extra toes are called polydactyl cats. Polydactyl cats are common in populations along the East Coast of North America.

a trait to appear, the gene is called "recessive" – the gene for a longhaired coat is recessive. If a cat has both a dominant shorthair gene and a recessive longhair gene, the recessive longhair gene is "masked". The cat will be a shorthair – there is no intermediate effect (i.e. mid-length hair).

Sometimes genes mutate – their structure changes – and they produce a different trait. Some of these mutations can then be passed down to future generations. By using cats with desirable genetic mutations, breeders can create new breeds of cats – for example, with curly hair. However, many serious diseases are also caused by genetic mutation, and focusing on breeding within a very narrow gene pool to promote specific traits can result in the appearance of new diseases and disorders (pp.244–5).

DOMINANT AND RECESSIVE GENES

Cats with dark coats have at least one copy of the dominant dense pigment gene "D", which produces hair packed with pigment. The recessive form of this pigment gene, "d", reduces the level of pigment, diluting the colour of the cat's fur. So, for example, if two black-coated cats (both with two copies of the black-coat gene "B") each have one copy of the dense (D) pigment gene and one of the dilute (d) pigment gene, there is a one-in-four chance that they could produce a kitten with blue (diluted black) fur.

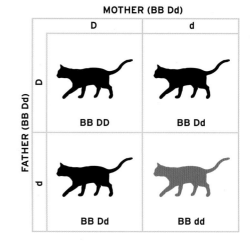

MOTHER (BB Dd)

FATHER (BB Dd)	D	d
D	BB DD	BB Dd
d	BB Dd	BB dd

A CAT IN BLUE
A "blue" cat has two copies of the recessive dilution gene. Cats possessing two copies of the dominant dense form of the gene - or one dense and one dilution gene - will have black fur.

Cat anatomy

The feline body-plan is that of a predator. The skeleton, which evolved for speed and agility, has slender limbs, a flexible spine, and a narrow ribcage to protect the heart and lungs, both of which are adapted for short bursts of speed. The shoulder blades are not attached to the rest of the skeleton but held in place by muscles and ligaments, allowing the cat to extend its stride when running.

A domestic cat's brain is about 25 per cent smaller than that of a wildcat. This is because the areas of a wildcat's brain involved in mapping a large territory are no longer needed by domestic

CAT'S WHISKERS
Whiskers are hairs that have been modified into touch sensors. They help cats to navigate in the dark and also to detect objects that are very close by.

EYES IN THE DARK
The large, wide-set eyes face forward for judging distances when hunting. Night vision is enhanced by the tapetum lucidum, *a reflective layer behind the retina that bounces any light entering the eye back through the retina.*

Ears can rotate independently to locate sources of sounds

Beneath the coat, the skin is usually the same colour as the cat's fur

A typical cat coat has an underlayer of soft, short hairs and mid-length insulating awn, overlaid by long, protective guard hairs

Front legs have greater range of movement than the hindlegs, allowing a cat to clean its head with its front paws

Paws have fleshy, hairless pads on their underside to provide support

CARNIVORE TEETH
An adult cat has 30 teeth. The incisors are used for grasping and grooming, the canines for stabbing and gripping prey, and the carnassials (modified molars) at the side for cutting flesh.

TOES AND CLAWS
Cats are digitigrade, which means that they walk on their toes. The toes have curved claws for scratching (which also sharpens them), fighting, and gripping. The claws are retractable: they can be slid back into sheaths for stealthy movement.

cats, which patrol much smaller ranges. Domestic cats are also a little smaller than their wild cousins.

Being carnivores, cats have a relatively short intestinal tract, because it is easier to digest meat than plant matter. A domestic cat's tract is a little longer than that of a wildcat. This reflects dietary changes – primarily the cereal content in food scraps scavenged from humans over millennia.

Cats have scent-producing glands in the skin around the mouth and tail, and also on the paws. They mark their territory using these scents and by scratching surfaces.

A cat's eyes are highly sensitive to small movements but their colour vision is poor, as cats are primarily nocturnal animals. Cats have a wider range of hearing than humans, enabling them to detect the high-pitched squeaks of rodents. In addition to acute senses of taste and smell, cats have a sensory organ in the roof of the mouth – the vomeronasal, or Jacobson's, organ. To use this organ, cats contort their face (an action called the "Flehmen response") as they pick up scents – usually those left by other cats. The several sets of whiskers on the face are highly sensitive to touch and air currents.

PREDATORY NATURE
Cats have evolved into superb hunters: they have sharp senses to detect their prey, a lithe, athletic body capable of bursts of speed to chase it down, and ferocious claws and teeth to catch and kill it.

COMMON FEATURES OF A CAT
All domestic cats have a similar design. Selective breeding has produced some variations in body size and shape, but almost all breeds are still recognizably close relatives of their wildcat ancestors.

A cat uses the position and movement of its tail to signal its mood

Powerful hindlegs propel a cat when running and pouncing

Legs are a little shorter than those of a wildcat

RIGHTING REFLEX
When a cat falls from a fence or tree, it has the innate ability – and amazing flexibility – to twist its body right-side up. As soon as it senses disorientation, the cat rotates its head, followed by its front legs, and finally the hindquarters. The soft pads of the feet and flexible joints help absorb the shock of landing. A fall or drop, however, can still prove dangerous to a cat.

Head turns

Front legs come round

Hindquarters rotate

Legs extend for landing

CAT BALANCING
The tail aids balance. Its highly complex range of muscles gives it a wide range of movement.

Body shapes

Eastern breeds, such as the Siamese, tend to have a slender and supple body with thin limbs and tail. This shape particularly suits a warm climate because it gives the body a large surface area, in relation to its volume, from which excess heat can be lost. Western breeds, such as the British Shorthair and most longhairs, are suited to temperate and cool regions. They tend to have a thickset, or "cobby", body with a stockier tail and limbs. In this instance, the shape minimizes the body's surface area and helps to reduce heat loss. Other breeds such as the Ragdoll, have a body shape somewhere between these two extremes.

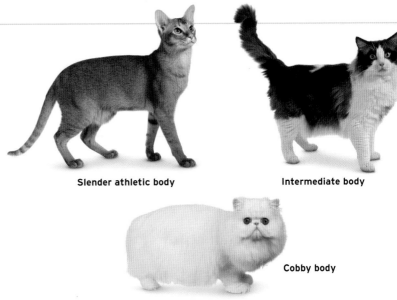

Slender athletic body

Intermediate body

Cobby body

Head shapes

There are three basic head shapes found in cat breeds. Most cats, including the British, European, and American Shorthairs, resemble their wildcat relatives, having a round head with a wedge-shaped face. In certain breeds, including the Siamese and the Devon Rex, the face has a much more elongated, or extreme, wedge shape. Other breeds, such as the Persian, are described as "doll-faced". In these breeds the cat's face is round with a flat nose, which sometimes causes breathing difficulties.

Rounded wedge face

Long wedge face

Rounded flat face (front)

Rounded flat face (side)

Tails

Most domestic cats have a long tail, although it is slightly shorter than that of their wild ancestors. The tail is used for balance and communication. In Eastern breeds the tail is often thin with an elastic quality described as "whippy". The defining characteristic of breeds such as the American and Japanese Bobtails and the Manx, however, is a short, stumpy tail – sometimes curved or kinked – or even a total absence of one. Another breed, the American Ringtail, has an unusual-looking curl in its tail; this is due to the cat's stronger-than-normal tail muscles, rather than any skeletal deformity.

Long tail

Bob tail

Ring tail

Eye colour and shape

Domestic cats have large, alluring eyes that come in a wide variety of orange, green, and blue tones. Some cats even have odd-coloured eyes, usually with one blue eye and one green or orange. Eye shapes can vary too, according to the breed of cat. Some breeds – for example, the Chartreux and the Persian – have round eyes, whereas others, such as the Maine Coon, retain the slightly slanted eyes of their wild ancestors. In some breeds of Oriental cat, including the Siamese, the slant of the eyes is even more pronounced, producing an almond-like shape.

Almond-shaped and blue

Slanted and green

Round and gold

Round and odd-coloured

Ear shapes

Almost all cat breeds have large, erect ears shaped like a half-cone, similar to those of their wildcat ancestors. In some breeds, such as the Siamese and Angora, the ear tips are pointed. Hair tufts at the tips, as in the Maine Coon, further accentuate the ears, so that they resemble those of a lynx. Other breeds, such as the British Shorthair and Abyssinian, have round-tipped ears. Two breeds have highly unusual ears caused by genetic mutations: the American Curl has ears that curl backwards away from its face towards the rear of the skull; in the Scottish Fold, a fold in the ear cartilage bends the ears down towards the front of the head.

Pointed tips

Rounded tips

Curled

Folded

Coat types

Coats are generally made up of three types of hair: down, awn, and guard. Soft, wavy down and fine, mid-length awn form an insulating undercoat, while the longer, stiffer guard hairs form a protective outer coat. The lengths and proportions of these types of hair vary among breeds, and not all breeds have all three types. Most cats are shorthaired, like their wild ancestors. Long hair is caused by a recessive gene. In Persians the hair may reach up to 12cm (5in) long. Curly, or "rexed", coats are caused by genetic mutations; there are now several rexed breeds, including the Cornish Rex and American Wirehair. There are also breeds, such as the Sphynx, with mutations that cause hairlessness.

Hairless

Short-coated

Curly-coated

Long-coated

COAT COLOURS AND PATTERNS

Cats come in a bewildering range of colours and coat patterns – there are endless combinations. Some breeds are defined specifically for their colour, such as the blue-only Chartreux, and others for just one kind of coat pattern, such as the pointed Siamese. In many other breeds any combination of colour and pattern is acceptable.

Coat colour is produced by two forms of the pigment melanin: eumelanin (black and brown) and phaeomelanin (red, orange, and yellow). Except for white hair, all colours – in solid and dilute forms – are derived from the varying amounts of these two pigments in the shafts of a cat's hair.

A cat's ancestral coat pattern is tabby. Selective breeding, however, has also created a wide range of other coat types, mostly produced by the expression of recessive genes. Popular patterns include "self", or solid-colour, coats,

pointed coats, smoke coats, and coats that have a mixture of colours, as seen in torties and bicolours.

White hair lacks pigment, and the white gene (*W*) is dominant over all other colour-producing genes and coat patterns. Therefore, cats with coloured and patterned coats have two recessive forms of the white gene (*ww*). Solid white is considered a Western colour (see below).

White coat

Western colours

Coat colours traditionally found in European and American cats, such as British Shorthairs, Maine Coons, and Norwegian Forest Cats, are known as Western colours. Specifically, they are black and red, along with their respective dilute forms, blue and cream. Bicoloured (a mixture of white patches and one of the Western colours) and self-white coats are often described as Western too. Today, Western colours have a global presence, having been successfully introduced into Oriental cats. Burmese cats, for example, are often bred so that their coats bear Western reds and creams.

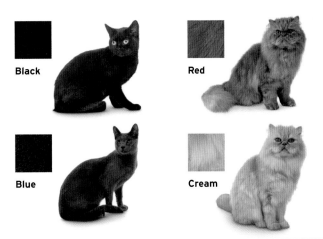

Black **Red**

Blue **Cream**

Eastern colours

Chocolate and cinnamon – and their respective dilute forms, lilac and fawn – are traditionally considered Eastern colours. These colours are thought to have originated in breeds such as the Siamese and the Persian. Nowadays, however, this separation of Eastern and Western colours is somewhat blurred, with cat colours having been transposed through breeding from one group of breeds to the other. All but the most conservative cat registries today accept Eastern colours in Western breeds, and vice versa. British Shorthairs, for example, are accepted in Eastern colours.

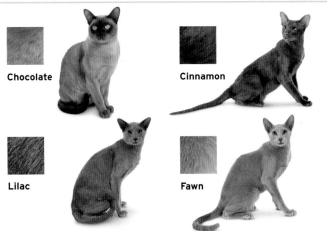

Chocolate **Cinnamon**

Lilac **Fawn**

UNDERSTANDING COAT COLOURS

■ **Pigmentation in cat fur** varies from an even distribution along the hair shaft, which produces a self (solid-colour) coat, to no pigment at all, which gives white fur. A self coat's colour is determined by the density of the pigment in its hairs. Dilute red, for example, gives cream. If just the end of each hair has colour, the coat is tipped, shaded, or smoke, depending on exactly how much of the shaft holds colour. Ticked shafts with alternating dark and light bands give a tabby colour called agouti.

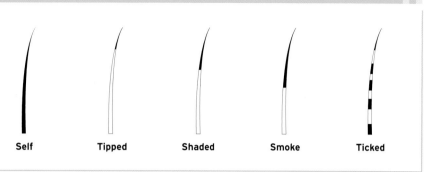

Self   Tipped   Shaded   Smoke   Ticked

Tipped fur

When just the very tip of each cat hair – about one-eighth of the overall length – is strongly pigmented, the effect is known as tipped, shell, or chinchilla. The rest of the hair's length is usually white (unpigmented), although in some breeds yellow or reddish colours have also been produced. Tipping is controlled by the interaction of several different genes. Some Burmillas, Persian Chinchillas, and Persian Cameos have tipped coats.

Light chocolate tipped

Blue-tipped silver

Shaded fur

In shaded coats the upper quarter of each hair shaft has colour. This pattern is produced by the same genes responsible for tipped fur but in shaded cats the coat appears darker on the back, where the fur lies flat. The heavier degree of tipping in shaded fur produces a dramatic rippling effect as the cat moves. Shaded coats are accepted and sought after in many breeds, especially Persians.

Cream shaded Cameo

Silver shaded

Smoke fur

About half of the hair shaft (the uppermost half) has colour in smoke fur. When still, many smoke cats appear to have a solid coat with just a paler neck ruff, but when the cat moves the lighter roots become more visible and the cat "shimmers". Smokes are very popular and are found in many breeds, including the Manx, Exotic Shorthairs and Longhairs, Maine Coons, and Persians. Smoke kittens are often difficult to tell apart from self kittens, as the smoke effect can take a few months to appear.

Black smoke

Blue smoke

Ticked fur

In ticked coats the hair shafts have alternating pigmented and paler bands (see box above). The tips of the hair shafts are always pigmented. Ticked fur is a characteristic of many wild cats and other mammals, and it provides good camouflage. Ticked, or agouti, hair makes up the lighter areas of tabby coats. A full, unpatterned agouti coat is a characteristic of Abyssinians and their longhaired relatives, Somalis. Abyssinians have 4 to 6 bands of colour on each hair and Somalis up to 20.

Silver sorrel

Usual

Particolours

Particoloured cats, or partis, have two or more definite colours in their coats. Partis include bicolour and tricolour cats and are found in many breeds, both shorthair and longhair. Partis also include torties (see below), with white spotting. Even a small amount of white counts as particolouring. When torties have a high proportion of white fur, the pattern is described as "tortie and white" or "calico". Particoloured cats are almost always female.

Particolour Ragdoll

Particolour British Shorthair

Tortie colours

Tortoiseshells, or torties, have distinct or mingled patches of black (or chocolate or cinnamon) and red fur. Variations include the dilute forms of these colours: blue, lilac, fawn, and cream. The pattern usually only occurs in females; on rare occasions the pattern may occur in a male, possibly due to a chromosomal abnormality. Torties with tabby markings are known as "tortie-tabbies", and these cats are classed as particolours (see above).

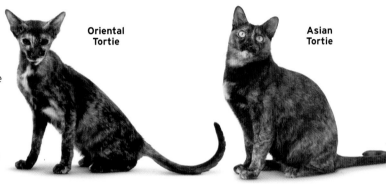

Oriental Tortie

Asian Tortie

Pointed

Cats with dark extremities and pale body fur are described as pointed. In Siamese and Persian Colourpoints this recessive characteristic is controlled by a heat-sensitive enzyme involved in producing hair pigment. The enzyme works only in the cooler extremities of a cat's body – hence the darker fur on the face, ears, paws, and tail. Other pointed patterns – such as the Van, in which colour is restricted to the ears and tail – are a form of white spotting (see below).

Self-pointed Siamese

Turkish Van

White spotting

The gene responsible for white spotting on a cat's coat is dominant. It works by suppressing areas of coloured fur to produce a coat that is bicoloured or tricoloured. The effect can range from almost totally white cats and the Van pattern (see above), to cats with just one or a few white patches in which the white fur is limited to the face, throat ("bib"), belly, and paws ("mittens").

Non-pedigree shorthair with white bib and mittens

White-spotted Maine Coon

Tabby colours

The ancestral pattern consists of swirls, stripes, or spots of solid fur – commonly black, brown, red (ginger), or silver (grey) – mixed with paler areas of ticked, or agouti, fur. It acts as natural camouflage for a cat – a definite advantage when hunting for food in the wild. The tabby pattern is a dominant characteristic and its various forms are still common not only in old breeds, such as the Maine Coon, but also in newer "wild-looking" hybrids, such as the Savannah. The Classic Tabby has a blotched or swirling pattern; the Mackerel Tabby has stripes, like a fishbone, running down its sides; and the Spotted Tabby has spots or rosettes. Tabbies have fine lines on their head (usually an "M"-shaped mark on the forehead) and barring on their tail and legs.

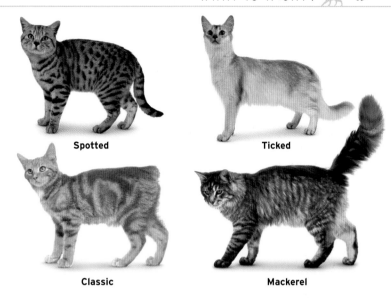

Spotted

Ticked

Classic

Mackerel

HOW TO USE THE BREED CATALOGUE

Catalogue entries will help you choose which cat is right for you. They outline the main features, appearance, and temperament of each breed, and specify any relevant care tips. At-a-glance data panels detail the origins, weight, and the breed registries that recognize the cat, along with the range of coat colours and patterns and the required grooming regime.

SINGAPURA

THIS SMALLEST OF CAT BREEDS HAS A KITTENISH TEMPERAMENT

Place of origin	Singapore
Date of origin	1970s
Breed registries	CFA, GCCF, TICA
Weight range	2–4kg (4–9lb)

Grooming

Colours and patterns
Sepia agouti: seal brown ticking on ivory ground colour.

The distinctive ticked coat of this little cat caught the eye of an American scientist, Hal Meadow, while he was working in Singapore in the 1970s. Meadow and his wife started a breeding programme for the Singapura, which they carried out both in Singapore and the USA. By the 1990s British breeders were also taking an interest in this cat. Singapuras are now known worldwide, although they are still very rare. Small in size but big in personality, these cats are prying and mischievous, happiest when exploring the world at a high level from a shelf or an owner's shoulder.

Dark facial markings on cheekbones

Long, strongly muscled legs

Sepia agouti coat paler on chin, chest, and underbelly

Large, deeply cupped ears

Enormous almond-shaped green eyes, set wide apart

Each hair of its fine, silky coat has alternate light and dark banding

Medium-long, slender tail has dark seal-brown tip

Firm, muscular body

Darker barring on inner forelegs and hind legs

BREED REGISTRIES

Abbreviations indicate which of the world's four major breed registries recognize this particular type of cat.

CFA The Cat Fanciers' Association, Inc.

FIFe Fédération Internationale Féline

GCCF The Governing Council of the Cat Fancy

TICA The International Cat Association

GROOMING KEY

The comb symbol and blue bar indicate how frequently you will need to groom this breed of cat in order to maintain its coat in top condition.

Weekly

2–3 times a week

Daily

CHOOSING THE RIGHT CAT

Cats make rewarding, lovable pets, but owning one can require a lot of time and money. If you think you would like to own a cat, you will need to do some research to make sure you are ready for the responsibility. If your heart is set on owning a pedigree cat, you will need to make sure you find a reputable breeder, though you may also be able to find a pedigree in a rescue home.

A pet cat can live for up to 20 years

Are you ready to own a cat?

Owning a cat might seem like a good idea, but you should give the idea serious consideration before you buy or adopt one. Consider if a cat will fit into your lifestyle. It is unfair on a cat to be left alone for long periods; they may seem independent, but cats need human companionship. Neglected outdoor cats may wander off, while indoor cats can become bored and destructive. It is not a good idea to get a cat if anyone in your household is allergic to cats or becomes asthmatic around them. Think carefully too if you have young children as you will need to spend time teaching them how to handle a cat.

Cats also mean changes to your home; you'll need to be able to cope with cat-hair-covered furnishings and the occasional half-eaten bird or mouse. You will also need to cat-proof your house, keep breakable items out of reach, and remove potential hazards such as houseplants that can be poisonous to cats (p.203). You will need to find somewhere to put your cat's litter tray, and get used to changing it regularly.

THE BEST BREED FOR YOU
Cat breeds come in many different sizes, coat types, and personalities. Do your research and work out which breeds will best suit your lifestyle – longhaired cats such as Persians (above) make beautiful companions but require a lot of grooming.

Cats can be expensive, and you need to make sure you can afford to cover the costs. There will be an initial outlay for your kitten or cat, which can reach hundreds of pounds for a pedigree. Advances in veterinary medicine and better understanding of a cat's diet mean that cats now live longer than they used to, even for as long as 20 years. The cost of owning a cat can add up to thousands of pounds over the course of its life. Pet insurance will help cover some veterinary costs, but probably not vaccinations, neutering, or dental treatment. You will also need to buy food, bedding, cat litter, and other accessories on a regular basis. If you go away, you will need to pay for your cat to stay in a cattery, or for someone to look after him at your home.

Deciding on a breed

If you would like a pedigree cat, make sure you do your research, so that you know about the breed's needs and characteristics. If you are unsure which breed to choose, you might want to consider size, coat type, and temperament. Breeds vary in size, between about 5 and 9kg (9–20 lb). Big cats are unlikely to take kindly to an indoor life in a small flat. If you want a longhaired breed, you will have to groom your cat every day, otherwise its fur will become matted; shorthaired cats generally need much less grooming (pp.228–31). Temperaments vary between breeds – Oriental cats such as the Siamese and Ocicat tend to be active and vocal, whereas heavier-set breeds such as the British Shorthair and Persian are usually quieter and more laid-back.

You should also think about what gender and age of cat will suit you. Male cats are usually bigger than females and may be more outgoing, but both make trouble-free pets once neutered. If you're worried about house-training a kitten, you could buy or rescue an adult cat. Finally, if there are stretches of the day when no one is at home, you might want to consider getting two cats, so that they can keep each other company.

NEW FAMILY MEMBER
Do plenty of research before you buy a cat or kitten, especially if you've never owned one before. A cat or kitten is a wonderful addition to the family, but can mean big changes in your routine.

Finding a breeder

Once you have decided which kind of cat breed you want, the best place to buy a pedigree cat is from a reputable breeder. You can find cats in newspapers, online, or in shop-window adverts, but generally these vendors should be avoided as they are not usually cat experts. It is also unadvisable to buy a kitten from a pet shop, as you will not be sure where the kittens have been sourced from. Your local vet may be able to recommend a breeder to you, or you could find breeders from a cat club list, breed registry list, or at a cat show – many of the people who show cats also breed them or will be able to recommend a breeder.

At the breeders, make sure you ask lots of questions, so that you know you will get a healthy, well-adjusted cat (see right). The breeder should also ask you questions, to make sure that you are responsible enough to own a cat and can afford to look after it. You should research the going rate for kittens of the breed you would like. A higher cost can sometimes reflect top quality and better care and attention

10 IMPORTANT QUESTIONS TO ASK A BREEDER

- How long have you been breeding cats for?
- Can I have references from your vet and previous customers?
- What are the important characteristics of this breed – will the kitten be "show quality" or "pet quality"?
- Does this breed suffer from any inherited diseases, and has the kitten been screened for them?
- How much time will I need to spend grooming?
- Has the kitten been socialized – will it be OK to introduce him to children and other pets?
- Will the kitten have been vaccinated and wormed by the time he's ready to be picked up?
- Have you registered the kitten with a cat registry, and can I have the printed pedigree?
- Can I have a written contract of sale, outlining both my and your (the breeder's) rights and responsibilities, and including an agreement that the purchase is subject to a vet's examination to check the kitten's health?
- Will I be able to contact you if I need advice after I bring the kitten home?

MEETING THE FAMILY
Kittens that have been socialized from an early age should not be timid or aggressive when encountering new people.

put in by the breeder. Some breeders offer "pet quality" as well as "show quality" kittens. Pet quality cats are just as healthy as show cats but have minor physical defects for the breed standard, and should be considerably cheaper than show quality cats. The breeder may ask you to sign an agreement not to enter pet quality cats in shows or to breed from them in order to keep breeding lines "pure".

It is important to meet the litter of kittens before you decide to buy one of them. A good breeder will let you observe the kittens and how they interact with their littermates. You should also meet the mother and check her health. She will give you an indication of your kitten's adult size, appearance, and temperament. The breeder may also own the father – if so, ask to see him too. The breeder can also give you an idea of the life span of the particular breed.

The kitten you choose to take home with you should appear healthy and alert, with a good muscle tone and a clean coat free from parasites such as fleas. His eyes should be bright, there should be no discharge from the eyes or nose, the ears should be free of wax, and the gums should be pink. Make sure your kitten has been (or will be) vaccinated, wormed, and screened for any genetic disorders that are known to occur in the breed. Take any certificates for these home with you if or when you buy a kitten. Avoid buying a kitten if it appears ill, if it has been kept in isolation away from the rest of its litter, if you think the kittens are being reared in substandard conditions, or if the breeder doesn't seem to know

A CAT WITH HISTORY
Many different types of cats end up in shelters. If you decide to give a home to a cat that is elderly or disabled, the rescue centre will sometimes help you to pay for its ongoing health care.

much about the breed or cat health care. If you're not happy, you can visit another breeder. If all goes well, you should pick up your house-trained, inoculated, and socialized kitten when it is about 12 weeks old.

Rescue homes

If you would like to give a home to a pedigree cat, one place you may not have thought of looking is in a rescue home, or shelter, for cats. Usually run on a non-profit basis, rescue homes are staffed mostly by volunteers and funded by private donations and adoption fees. They take in stray, unwanted, and feral cats and try to find suitable homes for them.

Pedigree cats can show up in rescue homes from time to time. Generally, these will be the more common breeds such as the Siamese, Maine Coon, or Persian – you are less likely to find an unusual breed.

After visiting a rescue centre and meeting all the cats waiting for homes, you may decide to adopt a crossbreed, or "moggie", rather than a pedigree cat. More than 95 per cent of all domestic cats are crossbreeds, and there are a large number of them housed in rescue shelters, each deserving of a loving home. Cat rescue centres are definitely worth investigating, especially if your preference is for a fully-trained adult cat with an established personality.

If you decide to adopt from a rescue shelter, a member of staff will visit your home to check that it's safe and suitable for a cat, and to make sure that you will make a good cat owner. You will be charged an adoption fee, which helps cover vet costs for rescue cats' health care, such as inoculations, blood tests, neutering, and microchipping.

RESCUE CATS
The staff at a rescue centre will assess the character of each cat and can help match you with your perfect pet; you may even find a pedigree cat in need of a home.

CATALOGUE OF BREEDS

SNOW BENGAL
Bengal cats are the result of crossbreeding between domestic cats and the Asian leopard cat. This Snow Bengal also has some albinistic genes, which accounts for its pale colouring.

SHORTHAIRS

Most cats have short hair, whether they are large or small, wild or domestic. This is an evolutionary development that makes sense for a natural predator relying on stealth and the occasional burst of speed. A hunting cat is more efficient in a short coat because it can glide unhampered through dense terrain and move freely for a lightning pounce in a tight corner.

A short coat keeps a cat warm without overheating

Developing the shorthair

The first cats to be domesticated, possibly over 4,000 years ago, had short hair, and their sleek-coated look has been popular ever since. In a short coat, colours and patterns are clearly defined and the feline form appears to full advantage. Dozens of shorthaired breeds have been developed, but there are three main groups: British, American, and Oriental Shorthairs. The first two are essentially ordinary domestic cats refined by decades of breeding programmes. They are sturdy, round-headed cats, with short, dense, double-layered coats. The strikingly different Oriental group have little to do with the East, being created in Europe through crosses with the Siamese. They have short, close-lying, fine coats with no woolly undercoat.

Other well-loved shorthaired cats include: the Burmese; the plush-furred Russian Blue, which has a very short undercoat that lifts the top guard hairs away from the body; and the Exotic Shorthair, which combines unmistakably Persian looks with a shorter, more manageable coat.

Short hair is taken to extremes in several hairless breeds, including the Sphynx and the Peterbald. These cats are usually not totally hairless – most have a fine covering of body hair with the feel of suede. Another variety of short hair is seen in rexed cats, which have wavy or crimped coats. Among the best known of these are the Devon Rex and the Cornish Rex.

Easy maintenance

A great advantage for owners of shorthaired breeds is that the coat requires little grooming to keep it in good condition, while parasites and injuries are easy to see and treat. However, keeping a shorthaired cat does not guarantee hair-free carpets and sofas. Some breeds shed quite heavily, especially during seasonal loss of thick undercoats, and even single-coated varieties such as the Orientals always lose a certain amount of hair.

ASIAN SELF
The Asian group of shorthairs are built on moderate lines, being neither cobby nor as ultra slim as the Orientals.

SIAMESE
The short, fine coat of the Siamese accentuates the elegant lines of this graceful blue-eyed cat. Many different point colours have been developed, but the classic seal point remains a favourite.

EXOTIC SHORTHAIR

A LOW-MAINTENANCE VERSION OF THE LONGHAIRED PERSIAN CAT

Place of origin	USA
Date of origin	1960s
Breed registries	CFA, FIFe, GCCF, TICA
Weight range	3.5-7kg (8-15lb)

Grooming

Colours and patterns
Almost all colours and patterns.

The first Exotics were bred in the USA in the 1960s, and by the 1980s there was a popular British version as well. These cats were created through breeding programmes that crossed the Persian (or Longhair) with shorthairs, including the Burmese (p.40), Abyssinian (p.83), British Shorthair (pp.68-77), and American Shorthair (p.61). Exotics combine the Persian's sweet, round-faced look and quiet temperament with a lush but short coat that requires minimal grooming. These gentle cats are happy as indoor pets and are always pleased to have someone around to play with or offer a lap.

Short, snub nose with distinct break between eyes

Flat face with full cheeks

Thick undercoat

Silver tortie classic tabby coat

Round head with broad skull

Small ears, rounded at tips

Huge, round eyes set wide apart

Stocky, deep-chested body is typically Persian

Soft, dense, shaded golden coat

Short, thickly furred tail

Short, sturdy, heavily boned legs

Large, rounded paws

KHAO MANEE

AN EXTROVERT AND INTELLIGENT BREED THAT IS EAGER TO DELVE INTO EVERYTHING

Place of origin	Thailand
Date of origin	14th century
Breed registries	GCCF, TICA
Weight range	2.5–5.5kg (6–12lb)

Grooming

Colours and patterns
White only.

The "white jewel", as the name translates, is a breed native to Thailand. Pure white cats apparently of this type are recorded in Thai history as early as the 14th century, but Khao Manees were not seen outside their native country until the late 20th century. Now they are attracting attention elsewhere, especially in the UK and the USA. This aristocratic breed has a palette of eye colours: it may have both eyes the same colour, be odd-coloured, have eyes the same colour but of varying shades, or even have eyes that are each bicoloured. Khao Manees are bold, friendly, and sometimes loud-voiced.

Odd-coloured eyes

Chiselled face with high cheekbones

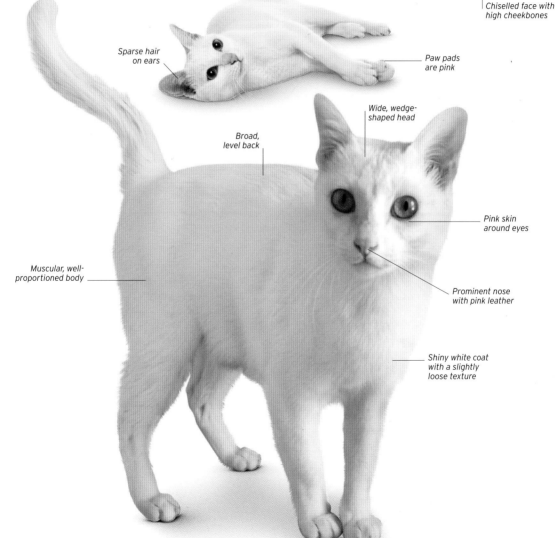

Sparse hair on ears

Paw pads are pink

Broad, level back

Wide, wedge-shaped head

Pink skin around eyes

Muscular, well-proportioned body

Prominent nose with pink leather

Shiny white coat with a slightly loose texture

KORAT

THIS ENCHANTING AND AFFECTIONATE CAT HAS A LONG AND PROUD HISTORY

Place of origin Thailand

Date of origin c.12th–16th century

Breed registries CFA, FIFe, GCCF, TICA

Weight range 2.5–4.5kg (6–10lb)

Grooming

Colours and patterns Blue only.

Few cat breeds can truly be described as being of ancient origin, but the Korat from Thailand is one of them. It appears in a book titled *The Cat Book Poems*, which dates back to the Ayudhya period (1350–1767), in what was then Siam. Long prized in its native country as a symbol of good fortune, the Korat was virtually unknown in the West until the mid-20th century, when a breeding pair was sent to the USA. This graceful, silvery blue cat makes a very special pet. Usually highly active, the Korat has its peaceful moments too, and is gentle and affectionate with its owners. With heightened senses, the breed is easily startled by loud noises or abrupt handling.

Large ears flare at base

Distinctive heart-shaped head

Oval paws

Lithe, muscular body

Very large, round green eyes

Close-lying, blue coat with no undercoat

Nose leather is heart shaped

Coat hairs are silver tipped

CHINESE LI HUA

A GOOD FAMILY CAT THAT NEEDS ROOM TO ROAM

Place of origin	China
Date of origin	2000s
Breed registries	CFA
Weight range	4–5kg (9–11lb)
Grooming	

Colours and patterns
Brown mackerel tabby only.

Cats fitting the description of the Li Hua, or Dragon Li as it is also called, appear to have been common in China for centuries. However, in the wider world this cat is a newcomer, recognized as an experimental breed only since 2003, although it is beginning to attract international interest. The Chinese Li Hua is a large cat with a muscular build and a beautifully marked tabby coat. Though not particularly demonstrative, it makes a friendly and faithful pet. This active cat, which has a reputation as a clever hunter, needs space to exercise and is not suited to a confined life in a small flat.

Lower jaw slightly shorter than upper

Black spot at corner of mouth

Long, straight nose

Straight, muscular legs

Lighter hair on belly

Ticked hairs form mackerel pattern

Bright yellow eyes

Sturdy, rectangular body

Tail has ring marks and black tip

Unticked beige hairs on chin and chest

ASIAN - BURMILLA

AN ENCHANTING COMPANION CAT WITH DELIGHTFUL LOOKS AND TEMPERAMENT

Place of origin	UK
Date of origin	1980s
Breed registries	FIFe, GCCF
Weight range	4-7kg (9-15lb)

Grooming

Colours and patterns
Many shaded colours, including lilac, black, brown, blue, and tortie, with silver or golden ground colour.

When the accidental mating of a lilac Burmese (p.39) with a Persian Chinchilla (p.140) in 1981 produced a litter of kittens with exceptionally beautiful coats, their owner was encouraged to experiment with further breeding. The result was the Burmilla, a cat of elegant Asian proportions, with large, appealing eyes and a delicately shaded or tipped coat; a longhaired version also occurs. Although still uncommon, this charming and intelligent breed is becoming increasingly popular. It possesses something of the zany character of the Burmese, modified by the quieter nature of the Chinchilla. The Burmilla enjoys games but will readily settle on a lap for a peaceful snooze.

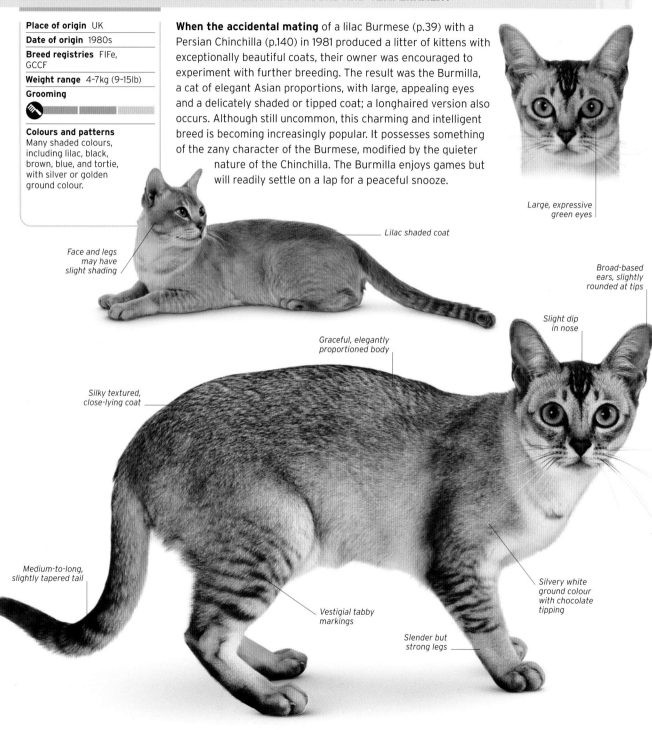

Large, expressive green eyes

Lilac shaded coat

Face and legs may have slight shading

Broad-based ears, slightly rounded at tips

Slight dip in nose

Graceful, elegantly proportioned body

Silky textured, close-lying coat

Medium-to-long, slightly tapered tail

Vestigial tabby markings

Slender but strong legs

Silvery white ground colour with chocolate tipping

ASIAN - SMOKE

THIS PLAYFUL AND INTELLIGENT BREED IS VERY RESPONSIVE TO ATTENTION

Place of origin UK

Date of origin 1980s

Breed registries GCCF

Weight range 4-7kg (9-15lb)

Grooming

Colours and patterns
Any colour topcoat, including tortie, with a silvery white undercoat.

Originally known as the Burmoire, this graceful cat is a cross between the Burmilla (opposite) and the Burmese (p.39). The Asian Smoke has one of the most attractive coats of all the Asian breeds: a deep, often solid colour on top, the fur ripples apart when the cat moves or is stroked to reveal glimpses of a gleaming, silvery undercoat. An athletic, playful cat with an outgoing personality, the Asian Smoke is highly curious and loves to investigate everything. Asian Smokes are happy kept as indoor cats as long as they have plenty of human companionship, amusement, and affection.

Chocolate smoke coat

Slender, well-muscled body

Tail tapers to tip

Strong, straight back

Medium to large ears, rounded at tips

Large eyes slant towards nose

Silvery rings around eyes

Wide jaw tapers to a blunt muzzle

Brown smoke with silvery white undercoat

Hindlegs longer than forelegs

Neat, oval paws

ASIAN – SELF AND TORTIE

LIVELY AND LOVING, THIS BREED IS VERY DEPENDENT ON COMPANY

Place of origin	UK
Date of origin	1980s
Breed registries	GCCF
Weight range	4–7kg (9–15lb)

Grooming

Colours and patterns
All self colours and various torties.

The result of experiments to create what is essentially a Burmese cat (p.39) with different coat colours, this British breed includes an all-black version known as the Bombay. The latter is easily confused with an American-bred black cat also called Bombay (p.36), which has a different breed history. The Asian Self may be less inclined to create an uproar in the household than its Burmese relation but can nevertheless make its presence known with an insistent voice when it wants attention, which is most of the time. This friendly, affectionate cat likes to follow its owner around with dog-like devotion.

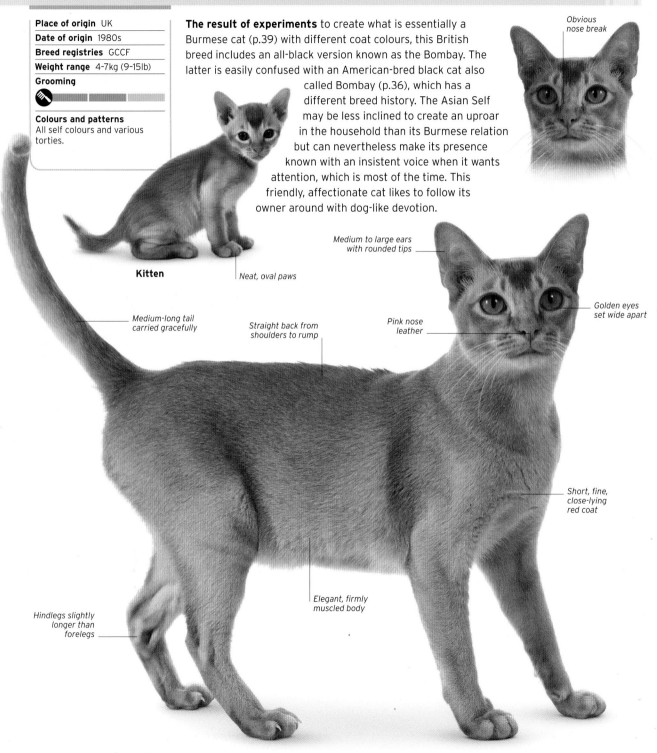

Obvious nose break

Kitten

Neat, oval paws

Medium to large ears with rounded tips

Golden eyes set wide apart

Medium-long tail carried gracefully

Straight back from shoulders to rump

Pink nose leather

Short, fine, close-lying red coat

Elegant, firmly muscled body

Hindlegs slightly longer than forelegs

ASIAN - TABBY

A SOCIABLE CAT THAT IS EASY TO KEEP IN A FAMILY HOME

Place of origin	UK
Date of origin	1980s
Breed registries	GCCF
Weight range	4–7kg (9–15lb)
Grooming	

Colours and patterns
Spotted, classic, mackerel, or ticked tabby patterns, in various colours.

This member of the Asian group of cats comes in four different tabby patterns: classic, mackerel, spotted, and ticked. The variety of stripes, swirls, rings, and spots occur in a wide range of beautiful colours. The most commonly seen pattern is the ticked tabby, in which each individual hair has contrasting bands of colour. Like all its relations, the Asian Tabby has the graceful, muscular lines and extrovert personality of the Burmese cats (p.39) used in its development, blended with the quieter nature of the Persian Chinchilla (p.140). This breed makes a lovely family pet and is growing in popularity.

Amber eyes with oriental slant

Short, thick, glossy, brown mackerel tabby coat

Prominent cheekbones

Delicate, oval paws

Medium to large ears set well apart

Blunt, wedge-shaped head

"M" marking on forehead

Straight-backed, muscular body

Rounded chest

BOMBAY

THIS PINT-SIZED "BLACK PANTHER" HAS GLOSSY FUR AND COPPERY EYES

Place of origin USA
Date of origin 1950s
Breed registries TICA, CFA
Weight range 2.5–5kg (6–11lb)
Grooming

Colours and patterns
Black only.

Created specifically for its appearance, the Bombay is a cross between the American Burmese (p.40) and the American Shorthair (p.61). Round and shiny, this breed comes only in black. It may look like a panther but it is a true homebody and few cats are more loving and sociable. Bombays want to be with their owners all the time, and are likely to mope if left alone for too long. Having inherited the inquisitive and playful nature of the Burmese, these cats are no couch potatoes. Bombays enjoy a game and are ready to be entertained. They get along well with children and other pets.

Head with softly rounded contours

Wide-set eyes are deep copper colour

Sturdy, muscular body

Nose has moderate stop

Full face

Round-tipped ears tilt forward

Tip of nose slightly rounded

Broad, rounded muzzle

Coal-black coat has deep sheen

Rounded feet

NOT SHY
The lithe and gleaming Bombay is a cat that feels confident in company. This breed is prepared to make overtures to anyone who is likely to provide entertainment or a lap to sit on.

SINGAPURA

THIS SMALLEST OF CAT BREEDS HAS A KITTENISH TEMPERAMENT

Place of origin Singapore

Date of origin 1970s

Breed registries CFA, GCCF, TICA

Weight range 2–4kg (4–9lb)

Grooming

Colours and patterns
Sepia agouti: seal brown ticking on ivory ground colour.

The distinctive ticked coat of this little cat caught the eye of an American scientist, Hal Meadow, while he was working in Singapore in the 1970s. Meadow and his wife started a breeding programme for the Singapura, which they carried out both in Singapore and the USA. By the 1990s British breeders were also taking an interest in this cat. Singapuras are now known worldwide, although they are still very rare. Small in size but big in personality, these cats are prying and mischievous, happiest when exploring the world at a high level from a shelf or an owner's shoulder.

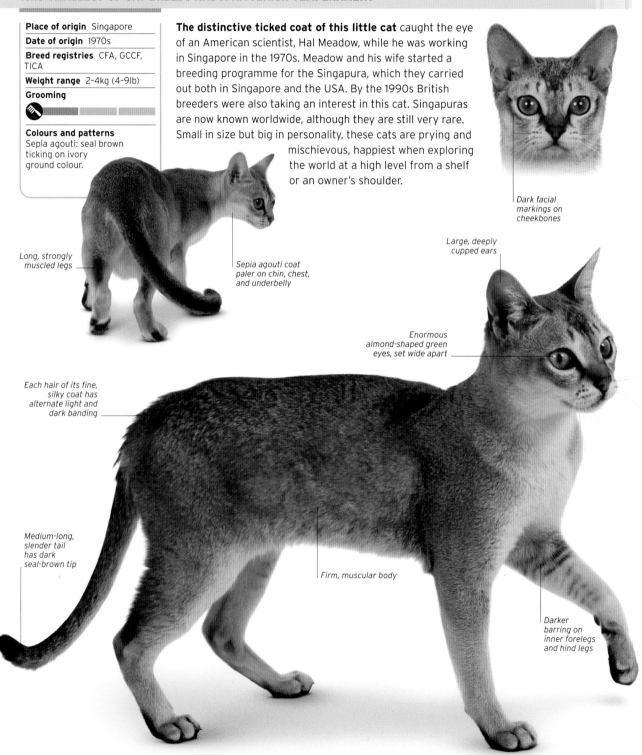

Dark facial markings on cheekbones

Long, strongly muscled legs

Sepia agouti coat paler on chin, chest, and underbelly

Large, deeply cupped ears

Enormous almond-shaped green eyes, set wide apart

Each hair of its fine, silky coat has alternate light and dark banding

Medium-long, slender tail has dark seal-brown tip

Firm, muscular body

Darker barring on inner forelegs and hind legs

EUROPEAN BURMESE

THIS CAT IS CONFIDENT, INQUISITIVE, AND FULL OF CHARACTER

Place of origin Burma (Myanmar)

Date of origin 1930s

Breed registries CFA, FIFe, GCCF, TICA

Weight range 3.5–6.5kg (8–14lb)

Grooming

Colours and patterns
Self and tortie colours include blue, brown, cream, lilac, and red. Always in sepia pattern.

This breed was first developed in the USA in the 1930s, using a foundation cat introduced from Southeast Asia. In the late 1940s several Burmese cats were sent from the USA to the UK, where the breed acquired a different look. The European Burmese is slightly longer in the head and body than its American counterpart, and comes in a greater variety of colours. This sweet-natured cat has plenty of affection to offer and needs to be a full member of a loving family. A Burmese is not well suited to a home where it will be left to its own devices for long periods.

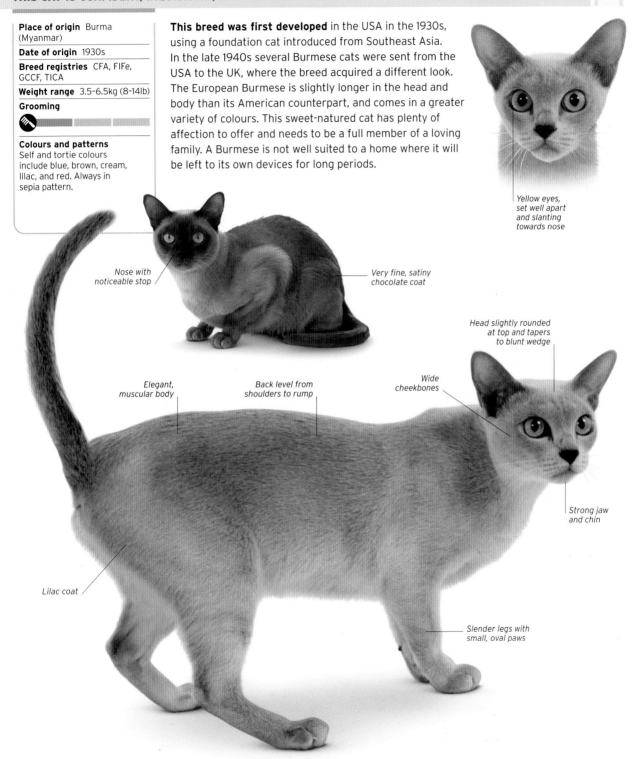

Yellow eyes, set well apart and slanting towards nose

Nose with noticeable stop

Very fine, satiny chocolate coat

Head slightly rounded at top and tapers to blunt wedge

Wide cheekbones

Elegant, muscular body

Back level from shoulders to rump

Strong jaw and chin

Lilac coat

Slender legs with small, oval paws

AMERICAN BURMESE

ALWAYS CRAVING COMPANY, THIS CAT IS FUN-SEEKING AND INTERESTED IN EVERYTHING

Place of origin Possibly Burma (Myanmar)

Date of origin 1930s

Breed registries CFA, TICA

Weight range 3.5-6.5kg (8-14lb)

Grooming

Colours and patterns
All self and tortie colours in sepia pattern.

There are several conflicting accounts of how the Burmese cat came to the West. All that is known for certain is that a Southeast Asian cat of this type, belonging to a Dr Thompson, appeared in the USA in the 1930s and was used to found a new breed. The first recognized American Burmese cats were all a rich brown in colour. Later, further colours were accepted, although not as many as in the European version of this breed, which also has a more Oriental appearance. The Burmese is a lovely family pet that can never have enough company and attention.

Visible break on nose

Wide-set, round golden eyes

Ears with slightly rounded tips

Full, round face

Richly coloured, close-lying lilac coat

Short, rounded muzzle

Underparts reveal lighter sepia patterning

Strong, compact body

Sturdy legs with round paws

MANDALAY

THIS GLOSSY-COATED BEAUTY WAS DEVELOPED FROM THE BURMESE CAT

Place of origin New Zealand

Date of origin 1980s

Breed registries FIFe

Weight range 3.5–6.5kg (8–14lb)

Grooming

Colours and patterns
Many self colours and patterns, including tabby and tortie.

In the 1980s two breeders in New Zealand discovered independently that accidental matings between Burmese cats (p.39) and domestic cats produced promising kittens. From these litters, they both went on to develop what is now known as the Mandalay, which has the same breed standard as the Burmese but a greater variety of coat colours. Sleek, glossy, and golden eyed, this lovely cat is best known in its native country. The Mandalay is very alert and active, and its lithe frame is packed with muscle. It is warmly affectionate towards its own family but inclined to be cautious with strangers.

Large amber eyes slant towards nose

Tail tapers very slightly to rounded tip

Strong, round chest

Top of head is slightly rounded

Back level from shoulders to rump

Wide jaw and firm chin

Short, black, satiny coat

Neat, oval paws

TONKINESE

A CHIC AND SLEEK BUT STRONGLY MUSCLED CAT WITH PLENTY OF SUBSTANCE

Place of origin	USA
Date of origin	1950s
Breed registries	CFA, GCCF, TICA
Weight range	2.5–5.5kg (6–12lb)

Grooming

Colours and patterns
All colours except cinnamon and fawn, in patterns including pointed, tabby, and tortie.

This hybrid cat, created by crossing the Burmese with the Siamese, blends the colouring of both breeds but has a more compact body than many cats of Asian ancestry. It has achieved considerable popularity both in the USA, where it was created, and in the UK. The Tonkinese has an independent spirit and would rule the household if it could, but it also has a loving nature and is gratifyingly eager to climb on laps. Playing games, socializing with other pets, and welcoming strangers to the home are all things that the Tonkinese is good at.

Slight stop on nose

Blunt muzzle

Brown shaded coat

High cheekbones

Darker brown legs, tail, and face

Round-tipped ears set to sides of head

Almond-shaped deep-coloured eyes

Well-balanced body, neither long nor stocky

Sleek, close-lying chocolate tortie coat darkens with age

Patterning continues into belly

Slender legs with oval feet

ORIENTAL – FOREIGN WHITE

THIS DAINTY ARISTOCRATIC CAT HAS A SPARKLING WHITE COAT

Place of origin	UK
Date of origin	1950s
Breed registries	CFA, FIFe, GCCF, TICA
Weight range	4–6.5kg (9–14lb)

Grooming

Colours and patterns
White only.

Development of this breed began in the 1950s, with crosses between the Siamese and white shorthaired cats. In the UK the first of these hybrids had either orange or blue eyes, but selective breeding produced cats with blue eyes only, which were given the name of Foreign White. Elsewhere, either green or blue eyes are permitted, and the cat is regarded as a self-coloured variant of the Oriental Shorthair, known as the Oriental White. This striking breed has the characteristic elongated lines and vibrant personality of the Siamese. Many blue-eyed white cats have a genetically linked tendency to deafness, but the Foreign White is free from this defect.

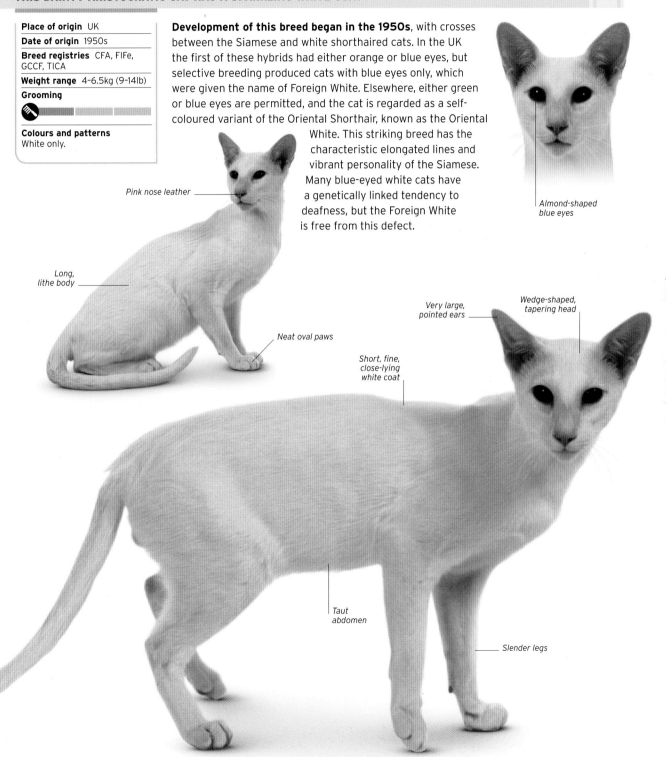

Pink nose leather

Almond-shaped blue eyes

Long, lithe body

Neat oval paws

Very large, pointed ears

Wedge-shaped, tapering head

Short, fine, close-lying white coat

Taut abdomen

Slender legs

ORIENTAL - SELF

THIS CAT WAS BRED TO COMBINE SIAMESE LINES WITH TRADITIONAL SELF COLOURS

Place of origin UK

Date of origin 1950s

Breed registries CFA, FIFe, GCCF, TICA

Weight range 4–6.5kg (9–14lb)

Grooming

Colours and patterns
Colours include brown (known as Havana), ebony, red, cream, lilac, and blue.

Self-coloured Oriental Shorthairs were developed in the 1950s, initially by crossing Siamese cats (pp.54-7) with other shorthaired cats to eliminate the typical Siamese colourpoint pattern. The first of the Oriental Shorthairs had coats in a rich dark shade of brown and were known as Havanas. In later years, these cats were used to develop a separate breed (p.52), in the USA. Decades of further selective breeding introduced a wide range of other solid colours to the Oriental Shorthair, starting with a dilute version of the Havana referred to as lilac in the UK and lavender in the USA.

Nose leather is pink

Lilac coat

Fine-boned but muscular body

Slightly slanting green eyes

Colour is uniform from root to tip of each hair

Long, straight nose

Long, elegant neck

Hips should not be wider than shoulders

Red coat has satiny texture

Hindlegs longer than forelegs

ORIENTAL – CINNAMON AND FAWN

THIS BEAUTIFUL CAT HAS TWO UNUSUAL COLOUR VERSIONS

Place of origin	UK
Date of origin	1960s
Breed registries	CFA, FIFe, GCCF, TICA
Weight range	4–6.5kg (9–14lb)

Grooming

Colours and patterns
Cinnamon and fawn with no trace of white.

These variations of the Oriental Shorthair are rare because it has proved difficult for breeders to produce their subtle colours. The first Cinnamon was a kitten born in the 1960s to a male Abyssinian (p.83) and a female seal point Siamese (pp.54–5). The attractive and unusual shade of this kitten's coat – a lighter, reddish-tinged version of the rich brown Oriental self-colouring known as Havana – inspired its breeder to develop a new line. Fawn Orientals, which were developed slightly later, are an even more diluted brown and their coats have a mushroom-pink or rosy tint, especially when seen in sunlight.

Vivid green eyes

Long, whippy thin tail

Typical Oriental body shape, lean and muscular

Colour of nose leather coordinates with coat

Fawn colouring has warm pinkish tinge

Fine, close-lying cinnamon coat

Long, slender legs

Dainty paws

ORIENTAL - SMOKE

THIS STRIKING CAT IS NOT YET AS POPULAR AS OTHER ORIENTAL COLOURS

Place of origin UK

Date of origin 1970s

Breed registries CFA, FIFe, GCCF, TICA

Weight range 4–6.5kg (9–14lb)

Grooming

Colours and patterns
Oriental self colours and tortie and patterns.

In 1971 a cross between a shaded silver hybrid cat and a red-point Siamese produced a litter of kittens in mixed colours. One kitten, which had the coat pattern known as smoke, inspired breeders to create a new-look Oriental. Each hair of a Smoke's coat has two colour bands. The top band may be either a self colour – including blue, black, red, and chocolate – or tortoiseshell; beneath this, the hair is very pale or white for at least one-third of its length. The pale hair shows through the darker colour and is particularly noticeable when the cat moves.

Vivid green eyes slant down towards nose

"Ghost" tabby markings

Ears with rounded tips continue wedge-shaped line of head

Long, tapering tail

Black smoke coat is short, fine, and glossy

Slender, graceful neck

Hindlegs longer than forelegs

Taut belly

Legs with same colour tone as face

ORIENTAL - SHADED

A DELICATELY PATTERNED CAT WITH AN UNUSUAL AND SUBTLE BEAUTY

Place of origin UK

Date of origin 1970s

Breed registries CFA, FIFe, GCCF, TICA

Weight range 4-6.5kg (9-14lb)

Grooming

Colours and patterns
All colours and tabby patterns, except white.

The chance mating between a chocolate-point Siamese (pp.54-5) and a Persian Chinchilla (p.140) produced a litter that included two kittens with shaded silver coats. This aroused breeders' interest and so began the slow progress towards a new range of Oriental cats. In a shaded Oriental, the coat is essentially a modified tabby pattern, in which the darker markings occur only on the upper ends of the hairs. These markings, which can appear as ticked, spotted, mackerel, or classic tabby patterns, may be quite pronounced in kittens, but as the cat matures the pattern becomes less distinct and in some cats is barely visible.

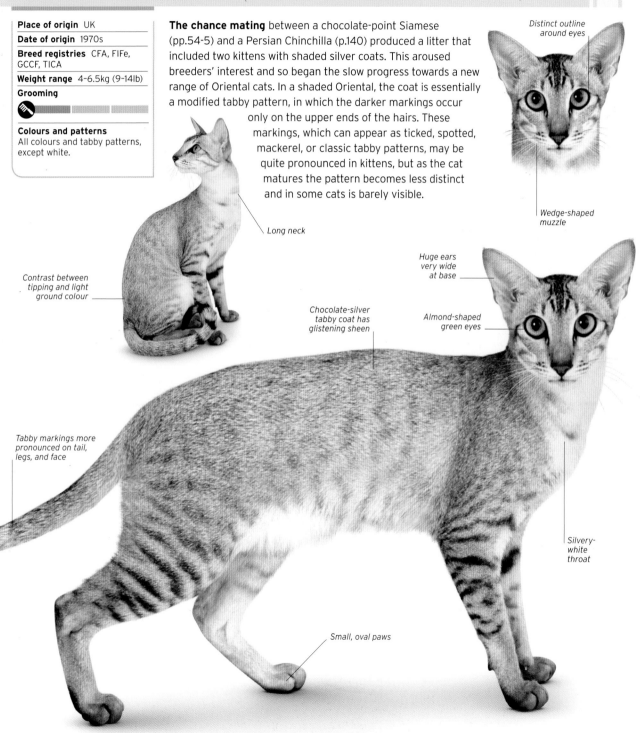

Distinct outline around eyes

Wedge-shaped muzzle

Long neck

Contrast between tipping and light ground colour

Huge ears very wide at base

Chocolate-silver tabby coat has glistening sheen

Almond-shaped green eyes

Tabby markings more pronounced on tail, legs, and face

Silvery-white throat

Small, oval paws

ORIENTAL STYLE
With its svelte body and striped or spotted coat, the Oriental Shorthair tabby has more than a touch of the jungle about it. All the traditional patterns and colours are accepted.

ORIENTAL - TABBY

THIS LIVELY CAT COMBINES STREAMLINED LOOKS WITH A RANGE OF BEAUTIFUL TABBY PATTERNS

Place of origin	UK
Date of origin	1970s
Breed registries	CFA, FIFe, GCCF, TICA
Weight range	4–6.5kg (9–14lb)

Grooming

Colours and patterns
All colours and shades in tabby and tortie-tabby patterns. Also with white.

Following the rising popularity of self-coloured Oriental Shorthairs, breeders turned their attention to producing a line of Oriental tabbies. Early attempts to introduce the tabby patterning to Orientals used crosses between non-pedigree tabbies and Siamese (pp.54-7). The first of these patterned Orientals, officially recognized in 1978, was a modern copy of the Siamese-type spotted tabbies believed to be the ancestors of today's domestic cats. By the 1980s Orientals with ticked, mackerel, and classic tabby patterning in a wide variety of colours had also been developed. The tortie-tabby Oriental, typically with patches of red or cream, was a further addition to the colour palette.

Green eyes

Lines run from top of head to back of neck

Rich brown markings on pale bronze ground

Black tortie silver-spotted coat

Large, blotched markings on flanks

Chocolate classic tabby coat

"Necklace" markings

Dark rings on tail

Belly lighter in colour

Barring on legs

ORIENTAL - TORTIE

THE PATTERNED COAT GIVES THIS CAT A PATCHWORK LOOK

Place of origin	UK
Date of origin	1960s
Breed registries	CFA, FIFe, GCCF, TICA
Weight range	4–6.5kg (9–14lb)

Grooming

Colours and patterns
Ground colours are black, blue, chocolate, lilac, fawn, cinnamon, and caramel; tortoiseshell pattern.

According to an illustrated manuscript, *The Cat Book Poems*, which may date back to the old kingdom of Siam (Thailand), tortie (tortoiseshell) patterned Oriental cats have a long history. Development of the modern Oriental Tortie began in the 1960s, with matings between self-coloured Orientals (p.44) and red, tortie, and cream point Siamese (pp.54–5). The breed eventually gained official recognition in the 1980s. The Tortie coat comes in several ground colours mingled with contrasting patches of cream, or red and cream, depending on the base colour. Due to the distribution of tortoiseshell genes, torties are nearly always females; the rare males are usually sterile.

Head narrows to a fine muzzle

Random-patterned coat

Chocolate tortie coat is warm brown mixed with red shades

Green eyes

Thin, tapering tail

Firm, medium-sized body

Fine bone structure

Dainty, oval paws

ORIENTAL - BICOLOUR

A LITHE AND SLENDER CAT WITH OFTEN DRAMATIC COLOURING

Place of origin	USA
Date of origin	1970s
Breed registries	FIFe, GCCF, TICA
Weight range	4–6.5kg (9–14lb)

Grooming

Colours and patterns
Various self colours, shades, and patterns, including tabby, tortie, and some colourpoints, always with white areas.

Breeders in the USA initially developed this exciting addition to the Oriental Shorthair group through crosses that included a Siamese (pp.54-7) and a bicolour American Shorthair (p.61). In Europe further programmes experimented with other crosses to achieve the "right" look. The first Oriental Bicolour in the UK arrived in 2004. This striking cat comes in a wonderful range of colours splashed over the coat in an endless variety of patterns; there is even a colourpointed, or Siamese, version. The breed standard requires the white patching to cover at least one-third of the cat and to include the legs, underside, and muzzle.

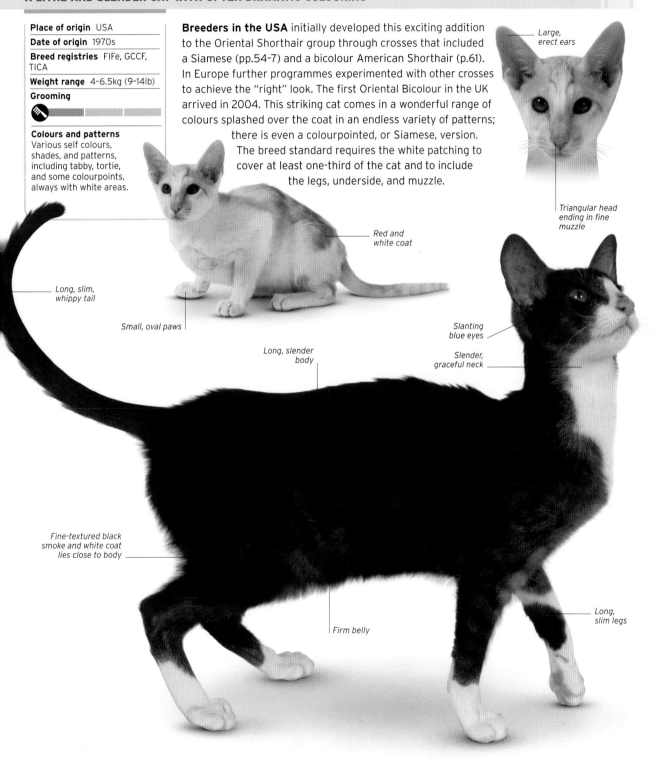

Large, erect ears

Triangular head ending in fine muzzle

Red and white coat

Long, slim, whippy tail

Small, oval paws

Long, slender body

Slanting blue eyes

Slender, graceful neck

Fine-textured black smoke and white coat lies close to body

Firm belly

Long, slim legs

HAVANA

A PLAYFUL, CHARMING, AND GENTLE CAT THAT ENJOYS AN INDOOR LIFE

Place of origin	USA
Date of origin	1950s
Breed registries	CFA, TICA
Weight range	2.5–4.5kg (6–10lb)

Grooming

Colours and patterns
Rich brown and lilac.

A rare breed with a confusing background, the Havana (originally known as the Havana Brown), was developed to have two different looks, both with a rich brown coat. In the UK the cat was produced through crosses with the Siamese (pp.54-7) and domestic shorthairs. This version, which had the long, lean Siamese conformation, was eventually classified as a self-coloured Oriental Shorthair (p.44). In North America breeders did not use the Siamese, resulting in a cat with a rounder face and less elongated body (shown here). The stunning Havana is hard to ignore, but if it does not receive attention it will certainly seek it. This affectionate cat likes to be close to people at all times.

Vivid green eyes

Muzzle narrows behind whiskers

Narrow head with rounded muzzle

Brown whiskers match coat colour

Firm, well-muscled body

Large, round-tipped ears

Sleek, rich chestnut-brown coat with no other colour markings

Brown nose leather has rosy tinge

Straight, slim legs with oval feet

THAI

THIS VOCAL CAT LOVES PEOPLE AND EXPECTS LOTS OF ATTENTION

Place of origin	Europe
Date of origin	1990s
Breed registries	TICA
Weight range	2.5–5.5kg (6–12lb)

Grooming

Colours and patterns
Any point colours, including tabby and tortie, with pale ground colour.

Lithe and elegant, with points that come in many colours, the Thai was bred to resemble the traditional Siamese cat of the 1950s, before it began to develop a more extreme, elongated appearance. The defining feature of the Thai is its head, which has a long, flat forehead, rounded cheeks, and a tapering, wedge-shaped muzzle. This cat is very active and intelligent, investigating everything and following its owner everywhere. It is good at communicating both vocally and in actions, and will persist in getting a response. The breed is not suitable for a home where it will be left alone for long periods.

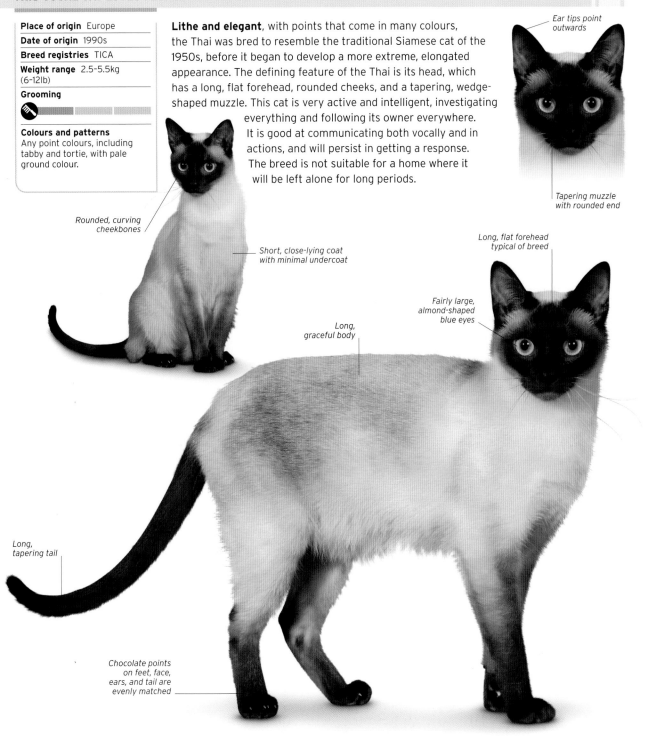

Ear tips point outwards

Tapering muzzle with rounded end

Rounded, curving cheekbones

Short, close-lying coat with minimal undercoat

Long, flat forehead typical of breed

Fairly large, almond-shaped blue eyes

Long, graceful body

Long, tapering tail

Chocolate points on feet, face, ears, and tail are evenly matched

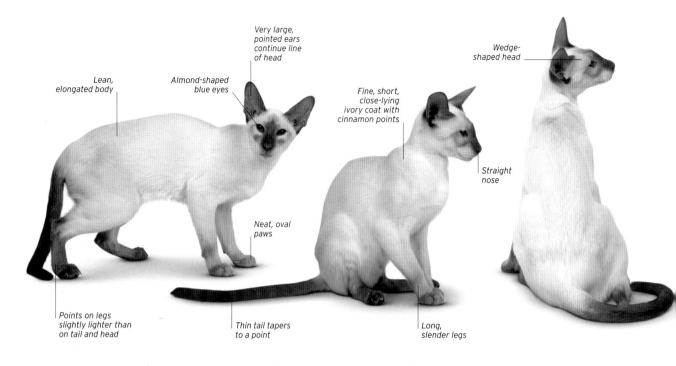

Lean, elongated body

Almond-shaped blue eyes

Very large, pointed ears continue line of head

Fine, short, close-lying ivory coat with cinnamon points

Wedge-shaped head

Straight nose

Neat, oval paws

Points on legs slightly lighter than on tail and head

Thin tail tapers to a point

Long, slender legs

SIAMESE – SELF-POINTED

THIS INSTANTLY RECOGNIZABLE BREED IS UNIQUE IN LOOKS AND PERSONALITY

Place of origin	Thailand (Siam)
Date of origin	14th century
Breed registries	CFA, FIFe, GCCF, TICA
Weight range	2.5–5.5kg (6–12lb)

Grooming

Colours and patterns
All self colours in pointed patterns.

The history of the Siamese includes more myths and legends than hard facts, and the true tale of this "Royal Cat of Siam" is now lost in time. It is certainly thought to be a very old breed; a cat with dark points is pictured in *The Cat Book Poems*, a manuscript produced in Siam (now Thailand) that possibly dates back to the 14th century. The first Siamese cats definitely known in the West appeared at cat shows in London during the 1870s, and in that same decade a cat was sent from Bangkok to the USA as a gift for the American president's wife.

In the breed's early years of development, on both sides of the Atlantic, all Siamese cats were seal points, and it was not until the 1930s that new colours – blue, chocolate, and lilac – were introduced, and later others were added. The appearance of the Siamese has also changed in other ways over the years. Traits such as crossed eyes and a kinked tail, which were once common in the Siamese, have been bred out and are now seen as

faults in terms of show standards. More controversially, modern breeding has taken the elongated body and narrow head of the Siamese to extremes, producing an ultra-lean and angular look. With a super-sized ego and a loud voice that it uses to demand attention, the Siamese is the most extrovert of all cats. This highly intelligent breed is full of fun and energy and makes a wonderful family pet, as ready to give affection as to receive it.

DEVELOPING COLOUR POINTS

All Siamese kittens are born pure white. Their point colours emerge gradually, and should be recognizable by around eight weeks. The colour may take a year or more to develop its full depth.

SIAMESE – TABBY-POINTED

THIS FRIENDLY BREED IS A STUNNING VARIATION OF THE WORLD'S MOST FAMOUS CAT

Place of origin UK

Date of origin 1960s

Breed registries FIFe, GCCF, TICA

Weight range 2.5-5.5kg (6-12lb)

Grooming

Colours and patterns
Many tabby point colours, including seal, blue, chocolate, lilac, red, cream, cinnamon, caramel, fawn, and apricot; also various tortie-tabby point colours.

A few Siamese cats with tabby points are mentioned in early 20th-century records, but selective development of this new variation did not begin until the 1960s. The first tabby point Siamese to attract the attention of breeders is said to have been a kitten born to a selfpoint female Siamese as a result of an unplanned mating. It was some years before the Siamese Tabby-Pointed was recognized and officially named as a breed in the UK; in the USA this cat is known as a Lynx Colourpoint. Originally, only seal tabbies appeared, but many other beautiful tabby colours have now been added to the breed standard.

Deep blue eyes

Nose leather pink with darker rim

Long, slender body

Dark-spotted whisker pads

Ears outlined in same colour as mask

Well-defined tabby stripes on mask, including typical tabby "M" mark

Ivory-coloured body with chocolate points

Faint stripes on legs

Tail has well-defined rings and solid-coloured tip

SIAMESE - TORTIE-POINTED

MULTICOLOURED POINTS ADD TO THE SPECIAL CHARM OF THIS SIAMESE

Place of origin UK
Date of origin 1960s
Breed registries GCCF, TICA
Weight range 2.5-5.5kg
(6-12lb)
Grooming

Colours and patterns
Various tortie point colours:
seal, blue, chocolate, lilac,
caramel, cinnamon, and fawn.

Producing tortie (tortoiseshell) colour points in the Siamese involves a complicated breeding process that introduces the gene for orange colouring. This gene causes random changes in self colours such as seal, blue, or fawn, resulting in a mottled pattern in which shades of red, apricot, or cream are evident. In some variations there may be striping as well. In kittens the full mixture of colours emerges gradually and may take up to a year to develop fully. The Seal Tortie-Pointed was the first colour to be granted official status as a Tortie Siamese in the UK in the late 1960s.

*Intensely
blue eyes*

*Delicate
muzzle*

*Long,
whippy tail*

*Large, pricked
ears follow
contours of head*

*Slender,
graceful body*

*Colour of nose leather
coordinates with points*

*Colour points
contrast with
ivory-coloured body*

*Pale coat with
seal tortie points*

*Each tortie
point is broken
up with cream*

COLOURPOINT SHORTHAIR

A LOVING, PLAYFUL CAT WITH A "LOOK-AT-ME" ATTITUDE

Place of origin USA
Date of origin 1940s/1950s
Breed registries CFA
Weight range 2.5–5.5kg (6–12lb)
Grooming

Colours and patterns
Various solid, tabby, and tortie point colours.

Developed specifically for its beautiful colour combinations, this breed was created during the 1940s and 50s, initially by crossing a Siamese with a red tabby American Shorthair (p.61). If not for its different range of colours, the Colourpoint Shorthair would be impossible to distinguish from the Siamese, as it possesses the same elongated body, slender head, outsized ears, and brilliant blue eyes as its relative. Intelligent, sociable, and highly vocal, this cat likes to be the centre of attention.

A Colourpoint Shorthair needs family life – the more fun going on, the better – and is not suitable for owners who are out of the home for long periods.

Deep blue eyes

Long neck

Clearly defined mask covers entire face

Finely boned, elongated body

Long, slender legs

Long, tapering, wedge-shaped head

Very large, broad-based ears

Short, fine, close-lying light coat with chocolate tabby points

Thin, tapering tail

Small, delicate paws

SEYCHELLOIS

THIS CAT IS NOT FOR OWNERS WHO LIKE A QUIET LIFE

Place of origin	UK
Date of origin	1980s
Breed registries	FIFe, TICA
Weight range	4–6.5kg (9–14lb)
Grooming	

Colours and patterns
White ground colour with self, tortie, and tabby contrast markings. Always bicolour and in pointed pattern.

This comparatively new breed, not yet recognized worldwide, was specially created in the UK to resemble the distinctively patterned cats found in the Seychelles. The first crosses were between a Siamese (pp.54–7) and a tortie and white Persian (p.152); later, Oriental cats were added to the breeding programme and the mix produced a graceful, long-headed, big-eared cat in both shorthaired and longhaired versions. According to the extent of its dramatic colour markings, the Seychellois is classified into three types, known as neuviéme (with the least colour), septiéme, and huitiéme (with the largest colour patches). With a reputation for scattiness, the Seychellois is said to be a demanding, although highly affectionate, companion.

Large, pointed ears

Deep blue, almond-shaped eyes

Wedge-shaped head with long, straight nose

Short, shiny coat with minimal undercoat

Strongly contrasting seal huitiéme markings

Long neck

Slim, elongated body with chocolate septiéme markings on coat

Long, thin, darker coloured tail

Long, slender, strongly muscled legs

Small, oval white paws

SNOWSHOE

THIS WELL-NAMED COLOURPOINTED CAT HAS DISTINCTIVE SPARKLING WHITE FEET

Place of origin USA

Date of origin 1960s

Breed registries FIFe, GCCF, TICA

Weight range 2.5-5.5kg (6-12lb)

Grooming

Colours and patterns
Typical Siamese colours in pointed pattern, with white feet. Blue or seal most common.

The white feet that define the Snowshoe were originally a "mistake", first seen in a litter of kittens born to a normal colourpoint Siamese. Their American breeder, Dorothy Hinds-Daugherty of Philadelphia, liked them enough to develop the striking new look, using crosses between Siamese (pp.54-7) and the American Shorthair (p.61) to produce the Snowshoe. Intelligent, responsive, and full of character, these cats love a home atmosphere and usually prefer to keep their family in sight. Most Snowshoes get on very well with other cats. Their steady temperament makes them a good choice for first-time cat owners.

Straight nose

High, rounded cheekbones

Light-coloured coat with seal colourpoints

Slightly rounded, wedge-shaped head

Large, broad-based ears have rounded tips

Walnut-shaped blue eyes

Close-lying, blue point coat with no undercoat

Long, athletic body

Long, white mittens on hind paws should be evenly matched

Oval paws

AMERICAN SHORTHAIR

A ROBUST, EASY-CARE CAT THAT IS RECOGNIZED IN A HUGE RANGE OF COLOURS

Place of origin USA

Date of origin 1890s

Breed registries CFA, TICA

Weight range 3.5-7kg (8-15lb)

Grooming

Colours and patterns
Most self colours and shades; patterns include bicolour, tabby, and tortie.

The first domestic cats in the USA are said to have arrived with the early pilgrims in the 1600s. Over the following centuries, sturdy, workmanlike cats spread all over America, most of them kept as efficient mousers rather than as house pets. But by the beginning of the 20th century, a more refined form of the farmyard hunter, known as the Domestic Shorthair, began to emerge. Careful breeding further improved the Domestic, and by the 1960s – now renamed the American Shorthair – it was attracting attention at pedigree cat shows. Healthy and hardy, American Shorthairs are perfect family cats that fit in with almost any type of household.

Broad, rounded head

Square muzzle and strong jaws

Short, thick, resilient coat

Round paws with heavy pads

Large head with full face

Ears slightly rounded at tips

Classic silver tabby coat

Well-developed, powerful body

Tail tapers to blunt end

Straight, muscular legs

INDEPENDENT SPIRIT
Either outdoor or indoor life suits the no-nonsense European Shorthair, a breed developed in Sweden. This young red tabby is fast growing into a typically robust and self-sufficient cat.

EUROPEAN SHORTHAIR

A FINE DOMESTIC CAT WITH AN AIR OF QUALITY

Place of origin Sweden

Date of origin 1980s

Breed registries FIFe

Weight range 3.5–7kg (8–15lb)

Grooming

Colours and patterns
Various colours and bicolours in self and smoke. Patterns include colourpoint, tabby, and tortie.

At first glance, the European Shorthair looks very much like a typical house cat. Largely popular in Scandinavia, it was developed in Sweden from ordinary domestic cats, but careful breeding programmes ensured that only the best foundation stock, selected for quality of colour and conformation, were used. Unlike most cats of similar type, including the British Shorthair, this breed has not been outcrossed to other lines. Robust and sturdily built, the European Shorthair is a dependable pet that thrives both indoors and out. It is sociable but retains an air of independence and can be a little aloof with strangers.

Blue eyes

Large, round face with well-developed cheeks

Nose straight and fairly broad

Thick, springy, cream-coloured coat

Firm, rounded paws

Muscular neck

Ears may be tufted

Medium-length, well-muscled and sturdy body

Very dense coat with blue shading

Rounded chest

Tail thick at base

Strong legs with even blue colouring extending to paws

Darkest blue pointing on tail

CHARTREUX

A CHUNKY BUT AGILE BREED WITH A "SMILEY" EXPRESSION

Place of origin	France
Date of origin	Pre-18th century
Breed registries	CFA, FIFe, TICA
Weight range	3–7.5kg (7–17lb)

Grooming

Colours and patterns
Blue-grey only.

Just how far back the history of this very old French breed goes is open to debate. The Chartreux was first named in the mid-18th century and some legends link it to the Carthusian monks, makers of the renowned Chartreuse liqueur, though there is no proof that they ever kept woolly coated blue cats like this one. With its calm, undemanding personality and soft voice, this breed is an unobtrusive yet affectionate house cat. It enjoys quiet play and occasionally explodes in a burst of extra energy when in a hunting mode.

Round head with full cheeks

Narrow, tapering muzzle with "smiling" expression

Blue-grey nose straight with slight stop

Short, dense blue-grey coat

Round golden eyes

Short neck

Weather-resistant coat is slightly woolly in texture

Blue lips

Body solid and muscular but not cobby

Sturdy, fine-boned legs

RUSSIAN BLUE

FRIENDLY BUT SELF-SUFFICIENT, THIS GRACEFUL CAT DOES NOT DEMAND MUCH ATTENTION

Place of origin	Russia
Date of origin	Pre-19th century
Breed registries	CFA, FIFe, TICA
Weight range	3–5.5kg (7–12lb)

Grooming

Colours and patterns
Blue of various shades.

The most widely accepted version of this breed's ancestry suggests that it originated around the Russian port of Archangel, just below the Arctic Circle. Supposedly brought to Europe by sailors, the Russian Blue was attracting interest in the UK well before the end of the 19th century, and had also appeared in North America by the early 20th century. With its gracious air and beautiful plush blue coat, it is not surprising that the Russian Blue is now highly popular. Reserved with strangers, this cat has an abundance of quiet affection to give its owners. Differently coloured forms of the breed have been developed under the name Russian Shorthair.

Dense fur gives broad-faced appearance

Straight nose

Thick, plush blue coat

Long, tapering tail

Long, finely boned legs

Long, lithe body

Relatively large, wide-set ears, very thin at tips

Bright green eyes

Silver-tipped guard hairs

Small, rounded paws

PLUSH FUR
The Russian Blue's coat, with its rich pile and silvery sheen, is a distinguishing feature of the breed. This kitten is still at the "cute" stage, but as an adult he will combine grace with dignity.

Large, powerful body

Short, dense black coat with no white markings

Small ears set wide apart

Large, round golden eyes

Short, strong neck

Massive head with full cheeks

Firm, round paws

Medium-short, strongly boned legs

Tail tapers slightly

BRITISH SHORTHAIR – SELF

A CAT THAT COMBINES GOOD LOOKS WITH AN EASY-GOING TEMPERAMENT

Place of origin	UK
Date of origin	1800s
Breed registries	CFA, FIFe, GCCF, TICA
Weight range	4–8kg (9–18lb)

Grooming

Colours and patterns
All self colours.

Originally developed from the best examples of ordinary British domestic cats, the British Shorthair was one of the first pedigree cats to appear in shows during the late 19th century. In the following decades the Shorthair was all but eclipsed by longhaired cats, particularly the Persian, but survived by a narrow margin to enjoy a revival from the mid-20th century onwards.

A descendant of cats that worked for their living, keeping down vermin on farms and homesteads, the British Shorthair is now something of a blueprint for the perfect fireside cat. The breed is highly popular in Europe and is steadily gaining a following in the USA, where it is less well known.

Many decades of careful selection have produced a well-proportioned cat of superb quality. Powerfully built, the British Shorthair has a medium to large, tightly knit body carried on sturdy legs. The massive, round head, broad cheeks, and large, open eyes are characteristic features of the breed.

The British Shorthair has a short, dense coat that comes in a variety of colours and has a deep pile and firm texture.

In temperament, this cat is as calm and friendly as its chubby-cheeked, placid expression appears to suggest. It can be kept equally well as a town or country cat. Strong, but not athletic or hyperactive, a British Shorthair prefers to keep its paws on the ground and is perfectly happy to stay indoors and commandeer the sofa. However, it also enjoys time outside and readily uses the hunting skills that made its ancestors such an asset in the past.

Quietly affectionate, the Shorthair likes to stay near its owner. Although alert to what is going on in the household, this cat it is not over-demanding of attention.

British Shorthairs generally have robust health and can be long-lived. They are easy to care for, as the thick coat does not mat or tangle and regular combing is all that is required to keep it in good condition.

BRITISH SHORTHAIR – COLOURPOINTED

SIAMESE-TYPE COLOURS ADD A NEW LOOK TO THIS TRADITIONAL BREED

Place of origin	UK
Date of origin	1800s
Breed registries	FIFe, GCCF, TICA
Weight range	4–8kg (9–18lb)

Grooming

Colours and patterns
Various point colours, including blue-cream, seal, red, chocolate, and lilac; also with tabby and tortie patterns.

The most recent of the British Shorthair variations, the Colourpoint was recognized only in 1991. This unusual cat is the result of experimental cross-breeding to produce a British Shorthair with the pointed coat pattern of the Siamese. Various attractive colours have been developed and, like the Siamese, all types have blue eyes, although the stocky build and round head typical of the Shorthair remain unchanged. Because of the similarities in name, the British Shorthair Colourpoint is sometimes confused with an Oriental-type American breed called the Colourpoint Shorthair (p.58).

Blue-cream
tortie mask

Pale
ground
colour with
blue-cream
highlights

Round
blue eyes

Chunky body

Typically full
rounded face

Powerful
shoulders

Tortie pattern
more evident
on tail

Short neck

Blue points
broken with
cream markings

BRITISH SHORTHAIR - BICOLOUR

THIS HANDSOME CAT IS BOLDLY MARKED WITH COLOUR PATCHES

Place of origin	UK
Date of origin	1800s
Breed registries	CFA, FIFe, GCCF, TICA
Weight range	4-8kg (9-18lb)

Grooming

Colours and patterns
Black and white, blue and white, red and white, and cream and white.

Black and white British Shorthairs were much valued in the 19th century when this breed had its beginnings, but they were never common. The Bicolour as it is today, which comes in several combinations of white and another colour, was not fully developed until the 1960s. At that time, almost impossibly high breeding standards required the colour patches to be distributed over head and body with complete symmetry. The rules have since been relaxed, but the best Bicolours still have strikingly even markings.

Pink nose leather

Solid-colour tail

Fluffy coat

Broad, rounded cheeks

Kittens

Large, rounded golden eyes

White blaze on face

Large, powerful body

Symmetrically distributed blue markings

Straight, well-boned forelegs

Rounded paws

White on legs and underside

CALM CHARACTER
This British Shorthair kitten, dozing off in mid-game, already shows the rounded cheeks that are one of the breed's characteristics. Although amiable, the Shorthair enjoys its own company.

BRITISH SHORTHAIR - SMOKE

THIS BREED'S HIDDEN SILVER UNDERCOAT CREATES A DISTINCTIVE EFFECT

Place of origin	UK
Date of origin	1800s
Breed registries	CFA, FIFe, GCCF, TICA
Weight range	4–8kg (9–18lb)

Grooming

Colours and patterns
Smoke pattern in all self colours, and in tortie and pointed patterns.

A Smoke cat can look as though it is just one colour, until it moves or its fur is parted to reveal a narrow silver band at the base of the hairs. This is the effect of the "silver" gene, which inhibits the development of colour in the coat, and which British Shorthair Smokes inherited from the silver tabbies in their ancestry. Smoke coloration is even more subtly attractive in the tortie version, which has two colours in the topcoat.

Round orange eyes

Black nose leather

Large, firm, rounded paws

Ears rounded at tips

Rounded forehead

Tail tapers to rounded tip

Prominent whisker pads

Black smoke topcoat conceals silver undercoat

Deep chest

Strong, medium to short legs

BRITISH SHORTHAIR - TABBY

AN OLD FAVOURITE THAT HAS BEEN DEVELOPED IN A VARIETY OF ATTRACTIVE COLOURS

Place of origin UK

Date of origin 1800s

Breed registries CFA, FIFe, GCCF, TICA

Weight range 4-8kg (9-18lb)

Grooming

Colours and patterns
All traditional tabby patterns with many colours, including silver variations; tortie-tabby in various colours, including silver variations.

Although the British Shorthair is the most even-tempered of cats, this variation is a reminder of its wild tabby-patterned ancestors. Brown tabbies were among the first British Shorthairs to appear in cat shows in the 1870s, and red and silver versions became popular early on in the breed's history.

This cat now comes in a wide range of additional colours, with three traditional tabby patterns: classic (or blotched) tabby, with markings arranged in broad whorls; mackerel, with narrower markings; and spotted. In the Tortie-Tabby, the coat has a second ground colour.

Typical tabby "M" mark on forehead

Brick-red nose leather

Vertical line runs down spine

Red classic tabby coat

Narrow markings on cheeks

Large, round golden eyes

Ground colour even over whole body

Even, unbroken rings on tail

Legs barred with darker bracelets

Necklace of stripes around neck

BRITISH SHORTHAIR – TIPPED
A DELICATELY COLOURED CAT WITH A SPARKLE TO ITS COAT

Place of origin UK

Date of origin 1800s

Breed registries CFA, FIFe, GCCF, TICA

Weight range 4–8kg (9–18lb)

Grooming

Colours and patterns
Various, including black-tipped on white or golden undercoat; red-tipped on white undercoat.

In a tipped cat a pale undercoat is overlaid with what appears to be a light dusting of colour. This effect is produced by the ends of the top hairs being coloured to about one-eighth of their length. The Tipped British Shorthair – originally called the Chinchilla Shorthair – comes in various colour forms. These include silver (white undercoat with black tipping), golden (warm golden or apricot undercoat with black tipping), and the rare red (white undercoat with red tipping), which is known as Shell Cameo in the USA.

Rounded muzzle

Red skin encircles copper-coloured eyes

Black tipping distributed over back, flanks, and head

White underparts contrast with red-tipped coat

Red nose leather outlined with black

Small to medium-sized ears

Black-tipped coat

Short, thick neck

Legs lightly tipped

Black-tipped tail with white underside

Body deep in flanks

BRITISH SHORTHAIR - TORTIE

MINGLED COLOURS GIVE THIS CAT'S COAT AN UNUSUAL MARBLED APPEARANCE

Place of origin UK

Date of origin 1800s

Breed registries CFA, FIFe, GCCF, TICA,

Weight range 4–8kg (9–18lb)

Grooming

Colours and patterns
Blue-cream, chocolate, lilac, or black tortoiseshell (with white patches in the tortie and white).

In a tortoiseshell (tortie), two coat colours are softly blended. There are many variations, but the most common is black mixed with red – the first tortie colour to be developed in British Shorthairs. Blue-cream tortoiseshell, in which black is replaced by blue and red by cream, is another of the older colours, recognized since the 1950s. In the Tortie and White (known as Calico in the USA) the colours are more clearly defined as patches. For genetic reasons, torties are nearly always female and the few males are sterile.

Deep orange eyes

White markings cover a third of the body

White paws

Areas of tortie patterning clearly defined

Red and black colour areas intermingle evenly

Dense tortie coat

Short, level back

Ears broad at base

Slight dip in nose

Broad chest

Rounded paws

TURKISH SHORTHAIR

A LITTLE-KNOWN BREED THAT IS AFFECTIONATE AND EASY-GOING WITH PEOPLE

Place of origin	Turkey
Date of origin	pre-1700s
Breed registries	None
Weight range	3–8.5kg (7–19lb)
Grooming	

Colours and patterns
All colours except chocolate, cinnamon, lilac, and fawn, and all patterns except pointed.

The history of the Turkish Shorthair is uncertain, but this cat occurs naturally in various regions of Turkey and has probably existed there for a considerable time. Also known as the Anatolian or Anatoli, and the Anadolu Kedisi in Turkey, the breed is similar to the longer-haired Turkish Van cat (p.176), with which it is often confused. The Anatolian is rare even in its native country, but breeders, particularly in Germany and the Netherlands, are working to increase its numbers. This strong, agile cat has a great liking for playing in or with water and is known to enjoy a bath.

Large, slightly almond-shaped eyes

Muscular neck

Tortie and white coat

Tail slightly rounded at tip

Moderately broad head with rounded jaw

Ears wide at base and set well apart

Short, dense tabby and white coat with no undercoat

Powerful, medium-sized body

Strong, muscular legs

Neat, round paws

OJOS AZULES

THIS RARE AND ENIGMATIC BREED IS A NEWCOMER ON THE PEDIGREE CAT SCENE

Place of origin	USA
Date of origin	1980s
Breed registries	TICA
Weight range	4–5.5kg (9–12lb)

Grooming

Colours and patterns
All colours and patterns.

First discovered in New Mexico in 1984, the Ojos Azules (the name means "blue eyes" in Spanish) is one of the rarest cats in the world. The stunning eye colour is particularly unusual in that it appears with any coat colour or pattern, in one or both eyes, including in the longhaired version. Currently, geneticists are monitoring the development of the Ojos Azules, as serious health problems, including skull deformities, have come to light. Because so few have been bred, little is yet known about the traits of this pretty and graceful cat, although it is said to be affectionate and friendly.

Nose has slight stop

Triangular head with prominent cheekbones

Sweet expression

Fine, silky white coat with black and red tortie markings

Odd-coloured eyes

Ears set relatively high on head

Square muzzle

Tapering tail with extensive tortie markings

Hindlegs slightly longer than forelegs

EGYPTIAN MAU

STRIKINGLY PATTERNED, THIS IS THE ONLY NATURALLY SPOTTED DOMESTIC BREED

Place of origin	Egypt
Date of origin	1950s
Breed registries	CFA, FIFe, GCCF, TICA
Weight range	2.5–5kg (6–11lb)

Grooming

Colours and patterns
Bronze and silver in spotted tabby pattern. Black smoke has "ghost" tabby markings.

This cat bears a certain resemblance to the long-bodied, spotted cats seen in the tomb paintings of Ancient Egyptian pharaohs, but it cannot claim direct descent. The modern Egyptian Mau was developed by Natalie Troubetzkoy, a Russian princess in exile, who in 1956 imported several spotted Egyptian cats to the USA from Italy. Here, the number of breeding cats remained small for many years, until new imports late in the 20th century reinvigorated the gene pool. Maus are affectionate cats but are also inclined to be sensitive and shy. They need thoughtful socializing at an early age and are probably best suited to an experienced cat owner. However, once a Mau bonds with its family, it stays devoted for life.

Medium-long, wedge-shaped head

Large, almond-shaped green eyes

Broad-based, fairly large ears

Bronze spotted tabby coat

Forehead has typical tabby "M" marking

Spots on coat are random

Hindlegs longer than forelegs

Loose flap of skin between flank and hindleg

Broken necklace patterns on upper chest and neck

Small, slightly oval feet

RARE BEAUTY
A silver Egyptian Mau stalks through long grass, huge green eyes fixed on a possible target. This stunning spotted cat, which comes in three recognized colours, is extremely rare.

ARABIAN MAU

A DESERT CAT THAT IS WELL ADAPTED TO HOME LIFE

Place of origin United Arab Emirates

Date of origin 2000s (modern breed)

Breed registries None

Weight range 3–7kg (7–15lb)

Grooming

Colours and patterns
Various self colours and patterns, including tabby and bicolour.

A breed native to the Arabian Peninsula, this cat was a desert dweller that migrated to city streets when human populations encroached on its habitat. In 2004 breeding programmes to develop the Arabian Mau were started, with the aim of preserving the cat's original traits and natural hardiness. With its high energy levels and need for mental stimulation, this breed can be a handful and will not be content to spend much time lazing around. However, the Arabian Mau is both loyal and affectionate, and sympathetic owners usually find it a highly rewarding pet.

Prominent whisker pads

Slightly slanted, oval eyes

Large, pointed ears

Spotted pattern continues on to underside

Nose slightly concave

Necklace markings

Long legs with oval paws

White self coat

Medium to large, muscular body

Banding on legs

Single mackerel tabby coat has firm texture

ABYSSINIAN

THIS SLINKY, GRACEFUL CAT IS FULL OF ENERGY AND NEEDS SPACE TO PLAY AND EXPLORE

Place of origin Ethiopia

Date of origin 19th century

Breed registries CFA, FIFe, GCCF, TICA

Weight range 4–7.5kg (9–17lb)

Grooming

Colours and patterns
Several colour forms, all with distinct ticking and facial markings.

There are various accounts of the Abyssinian's history, including the attractive but highly improbable story that it descends from the sacred cats of Ancient Egypt. A more plausible version suggests that its forerunners might have been brought back from Abyssinia (now Ethiopia) by British soldiers when the Abyssinian War ended in the late 1860s. What is certain is that the modern breed was developed in the UK, most likely by crossing the British Shorthair (pp.68–77) with a more unusual, and possibly imported, breed. With its athletic build, aristocratic bearing, and beautiful ticked coat, the Abyssinian is a striking cat with a hint of "wild" about it.

Intelligent and affectionate, Abyssinians make wonderful companions but they like an all-action life.

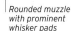

Rounded muzzle with prominent whisker pads

Distinctive dark facial markings around eyes

Silky, lustrous, usual coat

Eyes outlined in black

Large, alert ears set wide apart

Well-balanced, graceful body

Fine-textured blue coat

All hairs on coat are ticked with contrasting colour bands

Lighter underparts

Long, tapering tail

Slender legs

Relatively small paws

BRIGHT-EYED
All ears and eyes, even very young
Abyssinians are alert and perpetually
on the go. Almost everything engages
the interest of these hyper-intelligent
cats that need plenty of regular stimulus.

AUSTRALIAN MIST
THIS AFFECTIONATE CAT HAS A STEADY TEMPERAMENT AND A DELICATELY BEAUTIFUL COAT

Place of origin	Australia
Date of origin	1970s
Breed registries	GCCF
Weight range	3.5–6kg (8–13lb)

Grooming

Colours and patterns
Spotted or marbled tabby, misted by ticking; colours include brown, blue, peach, chocolate, lilac, and gold.

The first pedigree cat to be developed in Australia, this breed was created from crosses between Burmese (pp.39–40), Abyssinian (p.83), and Australian domestic shorthair cats. Formerly known as the Spotted Mist, it comes in a range of attractive spotted and marbled patterns and colours, all enhanced by ticking that produces a delicate "misted" effect. The Australian Mist is extremely popular in its native country and has earned a reputation as a particularly easy pet to keep. It has a loving nature, lives happily indoors, and is equally suitable as a playmate for children or a faithful companion for the less active owner.

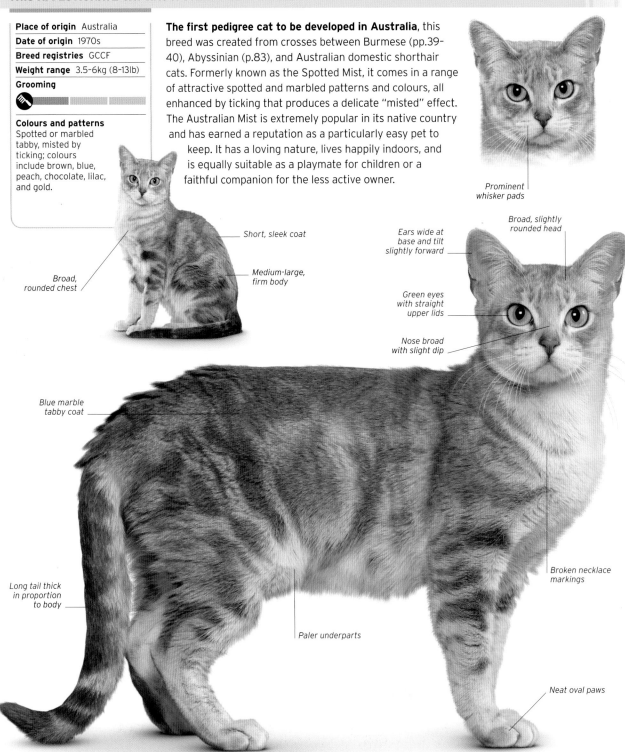

Prominent whisker pads

Short, sleek coat

Broad, rounded chest

Medium-large, firm body

Ears wide at base and tilt slightly forward

Broad, slightly rounded head

Green eyes with straight upper lids

Nose broad with slight dip

Blue marble tabby coat

Long tail thick in proportion to body

Broken necklace markings

Paler underparts

Neat oval paws

CEYLON

A FINE-BONED AND ELEGANT CAT WITH AN ATTRACTIVELY MARKED COAT

Place of origin Sri Lanka

Date of origin 1980s

Breed registries None

Weight range 4-7.5kg (9-17lb)

Grooming

Colours and patterns
Manila (black-ticked on sandy-gold ground colour); various other markings and tickings, including blue, red, cream, and tortoiseshell.

Named after its native home (now Sri Lanka), the Ceylon was imported to Italy in the early 1980s, where the breed was developed. It is now found worldwide and, if not as widely known as other breeds, has achieved some popularity in Italy. With its beautiful ticked coat and sandy colouring, this cat is similar in appearance to the Abyssinian (p.83), though the two are not related. The Ceylon has a distinctive pattern on its forehead called the "cobra" mark, which is much valued. Breeders praise the cat's friendly nature and its responsiveness to attention.

Distinctive "cobra" mark on forehead

Darker lines on cheeks and forehead

Yellowish green eyes with dark rims

Large ears set high on head

Well-defined stripes on legs

Necklace markings around throat

Kitten

Sandy-coloured, black-ticked coat

Clearly defined ticking on body

Broad chest

Short, fine-haired coat with minimal undercoat

Fine-boned but muscular legs

STRENGTH AND ELEGANCE
An Ocicat is a natural athlete, and the power in its graceful frame becomes evident when the cat is in motion. The sleek, spotted coat fits closely over smoothly gliding muscles.

OCICAT

AN ADAPTABLE AND CONFIDENT CAT THAT OFTEN RESPONDS WELL TO TRAINING

Place of origin	USA
Date of origin	1960s
Breed registries	CFA, FIFe, GCCF, TICA
Weight range	2.5-6.5kg (6-14lb)

Grooming

Colours and patterns
Black, brown, blue, lilac, and fawn in spotted tabby pattern.

Despite its name, this spotted beauty is not a cross between the domestic cat and the ocelot – the native jungle cat of South and Central America – but it looks as though it ought to be. The Ocicat was actually the surprise product of an attempt in 1964 to breed a Siamese (pp.54-7) with colourpoints that matched the ticked coat of the Abyssinian (p.83). The first spotted kitten that appeared was kept solely as a pet, but others produced later were used to create the new breed. The inclusion of American Shorthairs (p.61) in the Ocicat's development programme introduced greater size and substance. Ocicats have a delightful temperament, love company, and are easy to manage.

Broad, slightly
square muzzle

Silver-spotted
tabby coat

Characteristic
tabby "M" mark
on forehead

Large, almond-
shaped eyes
with dark rims

Lighter markings
around eyes
and on chin

Dark lines
on cheeks

Darkest coloration
appears on tip of tail

Powerful,
athletic body

Short, shiny chocolate
tabby coat marked with
"thumbprint" spots

Necklace
pattern
around neck

Long, slightly
tapering tail

Oval paws

OCICAT CLASSIC

A LARGE, BEAUTIFULLY MARKED TABBY WITH AN EXOTIC DIFFERENCE

Place of origin USA

Date of origin 1960s

Breed registries GCCF

Weight range 2.5–6.5kg (6–14lb)

Grooming

Colours and patterns
Classic tabby pattern in various colours, including silver.

A version of the Ocicat with markings in the classic tabby pattern rather than spots, this cat was recognized as a separate breed only comparatively recently, and is still not yet accepted as such by all breed authorities. The Ocicat Classic has the same history as its spotted cousin (pp.88–9), being a mixture of Siamese (pp.54–7), Abyssinian (pp.83–5), and American Shorthair (p.61). It is an energetic cat, with an enthusiasm for games and getting up on to high places. The breed has an excellent temperament and is highly sociable. An Ocicat Classic will not stay happy for long on its own, and is best-suited to a house full of people and action.

Large, broad-based ears

Long, broad muzzle

Large, almond-shaped eyes are angled slightly towards base of ears

Dark tabby markings on ticked brown fur

Traditional tabby "M" marking on forehead

Tail has dark rings along its length

Unbroken line of dark colour runs from shoulders along spine

Large, lithe, well-muscled body

Evenly spaced bracelet markings on legs

SOKOKE

THIS CAT HAS A PEACEFUL NATURE BUT IS POSSESSIVE OF HOME AND FAMILY

Place of origin Kenya

Date of origin 1970s (modern breed)

Breed registries FIFe, TICA

Weight range 3.5–6.5kg (8–14lb)

Grooming

Colours and patterns
Ticked brown tabby only.

A native of the coastal Arabuko Sokoke Forest in Kenya, this spectacular tabby was discovered in the late 1970s, when a British Kenyan resident adopted two feral kittens with distinctive markings and used them for breeding. Sokokes were later imported to Europe and the USA, and new bloodlines were introduced in the 21st century. The modern Sokoke combines the traits of what are known as the Old and New Lines. These cats develop close family bonds, and some have a natural talent for communicating vocally with their owners. They remain fairly active beyond kittenhood and enjoy playing games.

Eyes outlined with black

Prominent whisker pads

Long, slender, fine-boned legs

Classic tabby pattern on coat is blurred by ticking

Large, broad-based, upright ears

Black tip to tail

Skull almost flat at top

Long, whippy tail has firm feel

Chinstrap marking on throat

Long hindlegs give a tiptoe gait

CALIFORNIA SPANGLED

THIS CAT WITH EXOTIC "JUNGLE" LOOKS HAS A FAR FROM FIERCE PERSONALITY

Place of origin	USA
Date of origin	1970s
Breed registries	None
Weight range	4–7kg (9–15lb)

Grooming

Colours and patterns
Spotted tabby; ground colours include silver, bronze, gold, red, blue, black, brown, charcoal, and white.

This designer cat is a miniature reproduction of wild cats such as the leopard and ocelot. It was created by a conservation enthusiast, Paul Casey, specifically to discourage the killing of wild animals for their fur. Casey reasoned that if people related spotted fur to their own pet cats they would feel distaste for the destruction of wildlife in the name of fashion. The California Spangled was bred by using a variety of domestic cats, and has no wild cat species in its make-up. Hunting and playing are what this active cat enjoys most, but it is also sociable, affectionate, and easy to handle.

Slightly rounded forehead

Wide cheekbones

Prominent whisker pads

Well-defined spots of various shapes, including round, blocked, and oval

Eyes slightly angled towards outer edge of ear

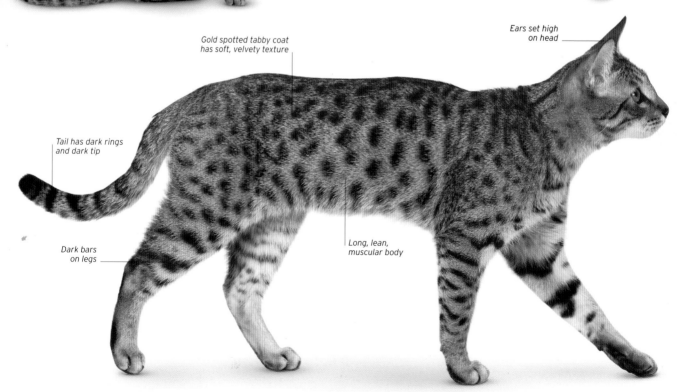

Gold spotted tabby coat has soft, velvety texture

Ears set high on head

Tail has dark rings and dark tip

Dark bars on legs

Long, lean, muscular body

TOYGER

THIS COMPANIONABLE AND INTELLIGENT BREED IS A STUNNINGLY BEAUTIFUL DESIGNER CAT

Place of origin	USA
Date of origin	1990s
Breed registries	TICA
Weight range	5.5–10kg (12–22lb)

Grooming

Colours and patterns
Brown mackerel tabby only.

A breed developed in the 1990s by crossing a striped, shorthaired cat with a Bengal (pp.94–5), the Toyger has a tiger-marked coat with random vertical stripes that are quite distinct from any other tabby pattern. Well built and muscular, this unique "toy tiger" moves with the flowing power and grace of a big jungle cat. The Toyger is confident and outgoing but has a relaxed attitude to life, which allows it to fit in well with any household. Although active and athletic, this cat is easy to handle and can be taught to play games and to walk on a lead.

Round eyes have deep colour

Long, broad head

Short, lush, glittery coat

Small, rounded ears are thickly furred

Kitten

Butterfly markings on head

Well-muscled neck

Long, strong body carried low to the ground

Long, muscular, low-set, ring-marked tail

Brown mackerel tabby coat

Powerful forequarters

Head longer than it is wide

Luxurious snow-spotted, dense coat is silky to touch

Body long and substantially built

"Mascara" markings around eyes

Round-tipped, relatively short ears with wide bases

Prominent cheekbones

Thick, low-set tail

Large, round paws

Strong, muscular legs

BENGAL

THIS CAT HAS A STRIKINGLY BEAUTIFUL SPOTTED COAT AND A VIBRANT PERSONALITY

Place of origin	USA
Date of origin	1970s
Breed registries	FIFe, GCCF, TICA
Weight range	5.5-10kg (12-22lb)

Grooming

Colours and patterns
Brown, seal sepia, and snow colours in spotted, marble classic, or pointed tabby patterns.

In the 1970s scientists crossed the small, wild Asian leopard cat with shorthaired domestic cats in an attempt to introduce the wild cat's natural immunity to feline leukaemia into the pet population. The project failed, but the resulting hybrid caught the interest of several American fanciers. In a series of selective breeding programmes, crosses were achieved between these hybrids and various pedigree domestic cats, including the Abyssinian (p.83), Bombay (p.36), British Shorthair (pp.68-77), and Egyptian Mau (p.80). The outcome was the Bengal, originally called the Leopardette, which was officially accepted as a new breed in the 1980s.

With its magnificently patterned coat and large, muscular frame, this cat brings more than a hint of the jungle into the living room. Despite its wild ancestry, there is nothing unsafe about the Bengal – it is delightfully affectionate – but it does have a lot of energy and is best suited to

an experienced cat owner. Friendly by nature, a Bengal always wants to be at the heart of its family, and needs company and both physical activity and mental stimulation. A bored Bengal will be unhappy and possibly destructive.

SNOW MARBLE CLASSIC TABBY

The Bengal's soft, short coat may be either a spotted or dramatic swirling marble pattern (as shown here). A snow-coloured coat usually indicates Burmese or Siamese ancestry.

KANAANI

THIS RARE BREED LOOKS LIKE A WILD DESERT CAT BUT HAS AN AFFECTIONATE NATURE

Place of origin	Israel
Date of origin	2000s
Breed registries	None
Weight range	5–9kg (11–20lb)

Grooming

Colours and patterns
Spotted and marbled tabby patterns with various ground colours.

Developed to have a close resemblance to the spotted African wildcat, the Kanaani is rare and many authorities do not yet accept it as a breed. Until 2010 the breeding programme for this cat allowed outcrosses with the African wildcat, Bengal (pp.94–5), and Oriental Shorthair (pp.43–51) – provided all these had spotted coats. Since then, kittens must have Kanaani parents only. With its big, slender body, long legs, and long neck, the Kanaani stands out as an unusual breed. This cat has a gentle and affectionate temperament but at the same time retains some of the independence of its wild ancestor and is also an excellent hunter.

Large, almond-shaped green eyes

Long, slender, muscular body

Spots softened by ticking

Black-tipped tail has at least three black rings

Characteristic "M" marking on forehead

Brick-red nose leather

Long, slim, muscular legs

Kitten

Large ears with tufted tips

Broad, triangular-shaped head

Long neck

Compact, oval paws

Short, coarse-textured, seal-spotted tabby coat

SAVANNAH

THIS TALL, GRACEFUL CAT HAS A STRIKINGLY UNUSUAL APPEARANCE

Place of origin USA

Date of origin 1980s

Breed registries TICA

Weight range 5.5–10kg (12–22lb)

Grooming

Colours and patterns
Brown spotted tabby, black silver-spotted tabby, black, or black smoke. Ghost-spotting may be visible in black or black smoke.

One of the newest cat breeds, the Savannah was officially recognized only in 2012. It originated from the chance mating of a male serval, a wild cat of the African plains, with a domestic female cat. The Savannah has inherited many of the serval's physical characteristics – including a spotted coat, long legs, and huge, upright ears – but is perhaps best known for its personality. This adventurous and athletic cat is permanently on the lookout for amusement, which might include playing with water, exploring the contents of a cupboard, or opening doors. As a Savannah can be quite demanding, the breed is not best suited to first-time cat owners.

Brow slightly hooded

Long neck

Long, slender, athletic body

Parallel stripe markings run from top of head along length of body

Extremely large, upright ears set high on head

Triangular head small in proportion to body

Brown-spotted tabby coat lies flat and has slightly coarse texture, though spots feel softer

Very long, muscular legs

Smaller spots on legs and paws

SERENGETI

TALL AND ELEGANT, THIS BREED HAS A GENTLE BUT OUTGOING TEMPERAMENT

Place of origin	USA
Date of origin	1990s
Breed registries	TICA
Weight range	3.5–7kg (8–15lb)

Grooming

Colours and patterns
Black self colour; spotted tabby in any shade of brown or silver (silver ground colour with black spots); and black smoke.

Designer-bred to resemble the serval – a small, leggy wild cat of the African grasslands – the Serengeti was created in California in the mid-1990s and is now also known in Europe and Australia. The result of crossing a Bengal (pp.94–5) with an Oriental (pp.43–51), this breed stands out among others with its long neck and legs, and upright stance. Most conspicuous are the Serengeti's exceptionally large ears, which are the same length as its head. This agile cat enjoys climbing and exploring high places. It bonds closely with its owner and is an ideal companion for someone who spends a lot of time at home.

Large, round eyes

Well-rounded whisker pads

Head longer than broad

Exceptionally large, wide-based ears with rounded tips

Long, lean, athletic body

Fine, dense silver spotted tabby coat

Long neck in proportion to body

Distinct, widely spaced spots

Very long legs

Dark tail tip

CHAUSIE

THIS SLENDER, SLINKY CAT HAS A CHARISMATIC AIR

Place of origin USA
Date of origin 1990s
Breed registries TICA
Weight range 5.5–10kg (12–22lb)
Grooming

Colours and patterns
Black self and ticked tabby pattern in brown and grizzled black.

Although the wild jungle cat and the domestic cat could, and probably did, interbreed naturally in the past, the Chausie originated from hybrids created during the 1990s. Initially, the jungle cat was crossed with a variety of cats, but today, to maintain consistency of the Chausie's shape and coat colour, only the Abyssinian (p.83) and certain domestic shorthairs are used. Like other hybrid cats, the Chausie is very active and enjoys exploring. It is intelligent and insatiably curious – a Chausie quickly becomes adept at opening doors to pry into cupboards. This cat requires an experienced owner who is able to spend plenty of time at home to provide companionship.

Eyes inclined to outer edge of ear

Long, high cheekbones

Ears have rounded tips

Round paws small in proportion to cat's size

Long head with sloping profile

Tall ears positioned on top of head and fairly close together

Large, lean, well-muscled body

Brown-ticked coat

End of tail has tabby barring and dark tip

Full whisker pads on muzzle

Long legs with faint barring on outer sides

MUNCHKIN

FRIENDLY AND SWEET, THIS SHORT-LEGGED CAT IS HIGHLY SOCIABLE

Place of origin	USA
Date of origin	1980s
Breed registries	TICA
Weight range	2.5–4kg (6–9lb)
Grooming	

Colours and patterns
All colours, shades, and patterns.

The first Munchkins were bred in Louisiana, USA, and although they are now achieving some popularity in America, in both shorthaired and longhaired versions (p.181), they are not accepted by many international breed organizations. The exceptionally short legs of the Munchkin, which arose as a random mutation, do not appear to affect speed of movement or longevity. This little cat may not have the jumping ability of its taller cousins but it still manages to climb on to furniture and is lively and playful. The Munchkin has been used to create other short-legged breeds such as the Minskin.

Flat forehead

High, well-defined cheekbones

Broad-based ears set on top of head

Rounded, wedge-shaped head

Slight nose stop

Black coat with white markings

Round paws

Fairly dense, weather-resistant lilac coat

Tail as long as body

Well-rounded chest

Legs about half the average length of other breeds

KINKALOW

THIS NEW AND RARE BREED IS SAID TO BE INTELLIGENT AND PLAYFUL

Place of origin	USA
Date of origin	1990s
Breed registries	TICA
Weight range	2.5-4kg (6-9lb)
Grooming	

Colours and patterns
Many colours and patterns, including tabby and tortie.

A designer dwarf cat, the Kinkalow was deliberately created in the 1990s by crossing the Munchkin (p.101) with the American Curl (p.109). This still-experimental breed ideally should have the small, compact body and ultra-short legs of the Munchkin combined with the turned-back ears of the Curl. Not all Kinkalow litters inherit these extreme traits, however, which are due to genetic mutations, and some kittens are born with both normal-length legs and straight ears. The development of the Kinkalow and the establishment of its breed standard are ongoing projects. So far, this miniature cat appears to be free from specific health problems and unhampered by its short legs.

Pink nose leather

Soft, sleek black coat

Curled-back ears inherited from American Curl

Silky red and black tortie coat

Short, compact body feels heavy for size

Tail long in comparison with body

White chest

Forelegs particularly short

SKOOKUM

DESPITE BEING ONE OF THE SMALLEST OF ALL BREEDS, THIS CAT IS FULL OF CONFIDENCE

Place of origin	USA
Date of origin	1990s
Breed registries	None
Weight range	2.5–4kg (6–9lb)

Grooming

Colours and patterns
All colours and patterns.

As a cross between the Munchkin (p.101) and the LaPerm (p.123), this little cat has inherited two striking features: extremely short legs and a soft coat, either long or short, that stands away from its body in exuberant curls or waves. The curly coat is not generally prone to matting and is easy to groom. The Skookum has been developed in several countries, initially in the USA, and also in the UK, Australia, and New Zealand. However, it is still rare and has not yet achieved universal recognition. This is an active, playful cat, able to run and jump just as well as longer-legged breeds.

Ears very wide at base

Walnut-shaped eyes look large for head

Slight stop between eyes

Sturdy body

Rounded, wedge-shaped head

Chocolate tortie tabby coat

Soft, springy curls stand out from body

Lighter coloured chest and underparts

Very short legs

Neat, round feet

LAMBKIN DWARF

THIS SWEET AND EASY-TO-KEEP CAT IS ACTIVE DESPITE HAVING VERY SHORT LEGS

Place of origin	USA
Date of origin	1980s
Breed registries	TICA
Weight range	2–4kg (5–9lb)
Grooming	

Colours and patterns
All colours, shades, and patterns.

This little-known hybrid dwarf cat is a cross between the short-legged Munchkin (p.101) and the curly coated Selkirk Rex (pp.124–5). It is sometimes known as the Nanus (meaning "dwarf") Rex. Still regarded as experimental, the Lambkin Dwarf is rare because it is extremely difficult to breed to type. In a single litter, some kittens may inherit both the mutant genes that pass on the short stature of one parent and the curly coat of the other, while other kittens may be short-legged and straight-haired, long-legged and straight-haired, or long-legged and curly-haired. These cats are reputed to have the docility of the Rex with a touch of the Munchkin's impishness.

Soft-textured coat

Very long tail

White-tipped tail

Pink nose leather

Pointed ears

Blue-cream tortie and white coat may have shaggy appearance

Hindlegs longer than forelegs

Body long in relation to legs

BAMBINO

AN AMUSING COMPANION WITH AN AFFECTIONATE, KITTENISH PERSONALITY

Place of origin	USA
Date of origin	2000s
Breed registries	TICA
Weight range	2–4kg (5–9lb)

Grooming

Colours and patterns
All colours, shades, and patterns.

This 21st-century experimental dwarf breed is one of the most extraordinary of all designer cats. Developed as a hybrid of the Munchkin (p.101) and the hairless Sphynx (pp.118–19), the Bambino is extremely short-legged with a heavily wrinkled skin that looks entirely naked, although it is usually covered with very fine peach-fuzz hair. Despite its dainty appearance, this cat is strong and athletic, with firm muscles and a sturdy bone structure. However, the lack of fur means that the Bambino is vulnerable to strong sun and low temperatures, and must be kept as an indoor pet. Grooming should consist of regular bathing to prevent a build-up of natural skin oils.

Large, round eyes

Strong neck

Short, firmly muscled legs

Well-rounded belly

Short, very fine downy hair has suede-like texture

Tapering, whip-like tail

Very large, broad-based ears

Pronounced wrinkles on head

Wedge-shaped head

Brittle whiskers are broken

Oval paws with long, slim toes

Short, broad, slightly curved nose

Unique ears fold downwards and forwards

Large, round golden eyes

Short, dense blue coat stands away from body

Short neck

Round, well-padded body

Neat, round paws

Fairly long tail tapers to rounded tip

SCOTTISH FOLD

A QUIET AND COMPANIONABLE CAT WITH UNIQUE FOLDED EARS

Place of origin	UK/USA
Date of origin	1960s
Breed registries	CFA, TICA
Weight range	2.5–6kg (6–13lb)

Grooming

Colours and patterns
Most colours, shades, and patterns, including pointed, tabby, and tortie.

Due to a rare genetic mutation, the ears of this breed fold forwards to fit like a cap over the skull, producing a unique round-headed look. The first Fold cat to be discovered was an all-white, long-haired female, known as Susie, that was born on a Scottish farm in the 1960s. At first, this cat and the folded-ear kittens she produced attracted only local interest, but then geneticists began taking notice and some of Susie's descendants were sent to the USA. Here, the breed was established, using crosses between Folds and British (pp.68–77) and American Shorthairs (p.61). During the development of the Scottish Fold, a long-coated version (p.183) also emerged.

These cats need careful breeding to avoid certain skeletal problems linked with the gene responsible for ear folding, and due to this risk they do not meet with the approval of all breed authorities. Scottish Folds are always born with straight ears that, in kittens carrying the folded-ear gene, begin to flatten forwards within about three weeks. Cats that remain straight-eared are known as Scottish Straights (see box). The Scottish Fold is still something of a rarity, more likely to be seen at shows than as a housecat. However, the breed is known for its loyal nature, and Scottish Folds that do become pets adjust easily to any type of family, making quiet and affectionate companions.

SCOTTISH STRAIGHT

Apart from having upright ears, the Scottish Straight looks the same as the Fold. Straights are barred from shows, but it is hoped that they will soon be recognized as a separate breed.

HIGHLANDER

THIS ACTIVE AND PLAYFUL CAT PROVIDES PLENTY OF FAMILY ENTERTAINMENT

Place of origin	North America
Date of origin	2000s
Breed registries	TICA
Weight range	4.5–11kg (10–25lb)

Grooming

Colours and patterns
All colours in any tabby pattern, including colourpoints.

This recently developed breed, which also comes in a longhaired version (p.186), is still extremely scarce. It has distinctive looks, with a big body, short tail, and dense coat. Most noticeable of all are the Highlander's large, curled ears; often thickly tufted, they add to the cat's air of wildness. Although not yet popular, the breed is beginning to earn recognition as a delightful housecat with a very special personality. Highlanders are ready to love everyone and make devoted companions. They have an irrepressible sense of fun, always want to play, and are said to be easy to train.

Wide muzzle

Well-defined whisker pads

Spots merge into stripes along top of back

Distinctive ears curl back loosely at tips, no more than 90 degrees

Large eyes set wide apart

Large, round paws

Broad, well-muscled shoulders

Broad nose

Short, thick tail

Brown-spotted tabby coat

AMERICAN CURL

AN ELEGANT AND ENGAGING CAT THAT MAKES A LOVING COMPANION

Place of origin	USA
Date of origin	1980s
Breed registries	CFA, FIFe, TICA
Weight range	3–5kg (7–11lb)
Grooming	

Colours and patterns
All colours, shades, and patterns.

The first American Curls were longhaired (pp.184–5) like the founding female of the breed, which was discovered in California. The shorthaired version was developed later and is essentially the same cat in a different coat. Big-eyed and elegantly proportioned, the American Curl is extremely attractive to look at. The curled ears, which may appear within a week of birth, add a touch of designer chic, although the mutation is an entirely natural phenomenon. This breed, noted for its sweet temperament, forms a close attachment to its family and always wants to know what is going on in the household.

Wedge-shaped head

Prominent whisker pads

Short, silky, brown-spotted tabby coat lies flat to body

Ears turn smoothly back at least 90 degrees

Large, brilliant eyes

Rectangular, moderately muscled body

Flexible, broad-based tail

Rounded paws

JAPANESE BOBTAIL
A CHARMING CAT WITH A BEAUTIFUL VOICE AND A UNIQUE POM-POM TAIL

Place of origin	Japan
Date of origin	c.17th century
Breed registries	CFA, TICA
Weight range	2.5–4kg (6–9lb)
Grooming	

Colours and patterns
All colours and patterns, including tabby (except ticked), tortie, and bicolour.

In its native Japan this cat is said to bring good luck and is a popular subject for ceramic ornaments. The Japanese Bobtail was spotted in the 1960s by an American enthusiast, who sent a number of the cats to the USA to begin a breeding programme. This shorthaired version won recognition in the late 1970s, followed a decade or so later by the longhaired version (p.188). An attractive and beautifully proportioned cat, the Japanese Bobtail is outgoing and intelligent. It has a charmingly melodious voice and fond owners like to claim that it talks, or even sings, to them.

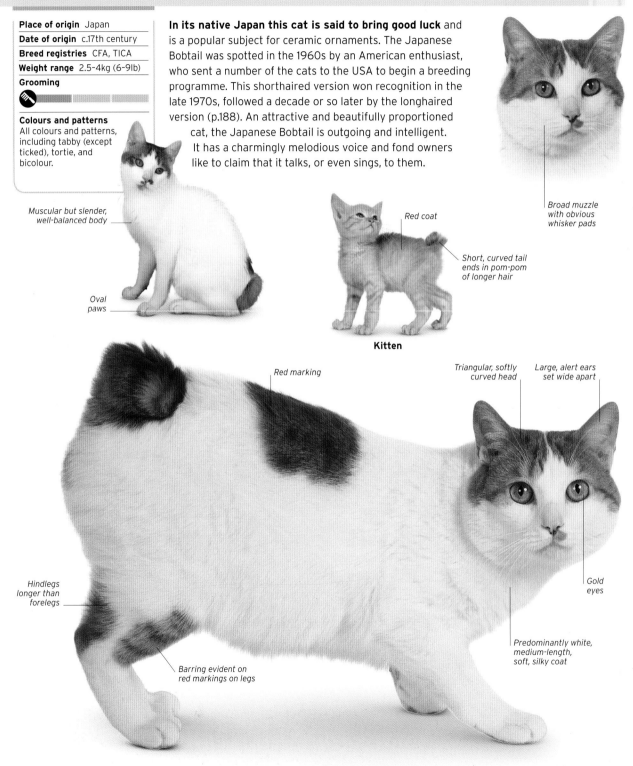

Broad muzzle with obvious whisker pads

Muscular but slender, well-balanced body

Oval paws

Red coat

Short, curved tail ends in pom-pom of longer hair

Kitten

Red marking

Triangular, softly curved head

Large, alert ears set wide apart

Gold eyes

Hindlegs longer than forelegs

Barring evident on red markings on legs

Predominantly white, medium-length, soft, silky coat

KURILIAN BOBTAIL
THIS STURDY AND STRONG-LIMBED CAT HAS A QUIRKY TAIL

Place of origin Kuril Islands, North Pacific

Date of origin 20th century

Breed registries FIFe, TICA

Weight range 3–4.5kg (7–10lb)

Grooming

Colours and patterns
Most self colours and shades in bicolour, tortie, and tabby (except ticked) patterns.

Native to the Kuril Islands, which form a chain between the North Pacific and the Sea of Okhotsk, off Siberia, the Kurilian Bobtail first became popular as a domestic cat in mainland Russia during the 20th century. Since the 1990s this breed, in longhaired (p.189) as well as shorthaired versions, has also been appearing regularly at Russian cat shows but it is little known elsewhere. The curious tail is a natural mutation and differs from one cat to another; it always has a number of kinks and may curl or bend in almost any direction. Kurilian Bobtails are relaxed, sociable cats, and said to be superb mousers.

Slightly angled, large eyes

Broad, straight nose

Short, kinked tail at least two vertebrae long

Triangular ears tilt slightly forward

Close-lying brown mackerel tabby coat has minimal undercoat

Well-muscled, compact body

Broad, slightly rounded chin

Strong legs with solid bone structure

Well-developed thighs

MEKONG BOBTAIL

THIS LITTLE-KNOWN BREED HAS AN ATTRACTIVE SIAMESE-POINTED COAT

Place of origin Southeast Asia

Date of origin Pre-20th century

Breed registries Other

Weight range 3.5–6kg (8–13lb)

Grooming

Colours and patterns
Colourpoints as Siamese (pp.54–7).

Named after the great Mekong River that flows through China, Laos, Cambodia, and Vietnam, this short-tailed cat occurs naturally over a wide area of Southeast Asia. The Mekong Bobtail was developed as an experimental breed in Russia and has been recognized by some authorities since 2004, although worldwide it is not particularly well known. It is a strongly built cat with the brilliant blue eyes and colourpointed coat of a Siamese. The Mekong Bobtail is active and agile, and is good at jumping and climbing. It is said to be a quiet breed with a friendly, well-balanced personality.

Prominent cheekbones

Short, glossy coat with minimal undercoat

Medium, broad-based ears

Large, almond-shaped, bright blue eyes

Solidly built, medium-size, rectangular body

Short, kinked tail

Hindlegs longer than forelegs

Cream coat with chocolate pointing

Legs slender in comparison with body

Oval paws

AMERICAN BOBTAIL

BIG AND BEAUTIFUL, THIS CAT IS AN EXCELLENT AND HIGHLY ADAPTABLE COMPANION

Place of origin	USA
Date of origin	1960s
Breed registries	CFA, TICA
Weight range	3–7kg (7–15lb)

Grooming

Colours and patterns
All colours, shades, and patterns, including tabby, tortie, and colourpoint.

The breeding of domestic bobtail cats native to the USA has been reported several times since about the middle of the 20th century, but so far only this one has been fully recognized. There is also a longer-haired version (p.193), and both types have the naturally occurring shortened tail that gives the breed its name. The American Bobtail is a substantially built cat, with powerful muscles and large bones. It is intelligent, alert, and reasonably active but also enjoys quiet times. This cat is happy to be among people, without overwhelming them with its attentions, and fits in comfortably with any type of household.

Broad, wedge-shaped head

Muzzle slightly wider than long

Semi-dense, medium-short coat has soft undercoat

Large whisker pads

Tufted ears with slightly rounded tips

Distinctive heavy brow

Nose wide with large leather

Moderately long, powerful body

Broad-based tail with seal pointing

Deep flanks

Tabby markings on legs

Large, round paws

TAIL TYPES
Manx cats are classified according to tail length. Categories include "rumpy" (completely tailless); "stumpy" (the tail has from one to three vertebrae); and "longy" (the tail is almost normal length).

MANX

BEST KNOWN OF THE TAILLESS CATS, THIS BREED IS POPULAR FOR ITS QUIET CHARM

Place of origin	UK
Date of origin	Pre-18th century
Breed registries	CFA, FIFe, GCCF, TICA
Weight range	3.5–5.5kg (8–12lb)

Grooming

Colours and patterns
All colours, shades, and patterns, including tabby and tortie.

Few breeds have as many stories about their origins as the tailless Manx. Among the more nonsensical legends, this cat is supposed to have lost its tail in an accident on Noah's Ark. In reality, it is native to the Isle of Man, in the Irish Sea, and its lack of tail is a natural mutation. The Manx has interested cat fanciers since the early 20th century and, together with its long-haired relation, the Cymric (p.192), is known worldwide. Breeding is carefully controlled to avoid the spinal problems sometimes associated with tailless cats. The Manx is gentle and calm, and can be trained to play "fetch" or walk on a lead.

Tortoiseshell and white coat

Red classic tabby coat has clearly delineated texture

White paws

Short tail stump

Rump has characteristic rounded appearance

Round head with full cheeks

Eyes angled slightly towards nose

Large whisker pads

Heavily muscled hindlegs much longer than forelegs

Sturdy, compact body with deep flanks

Heavily boned legs

Kitten

PIXIEBOB

HEFTY AND MUSCULAR, THIS CAT LOOKS FIERCE BUT HAS A SWEET TEMPERAMENT

Place of origin	USA
Date of origin	1980s
Breed registries	TICA
Weight range	4–8kg (9–18lb)
Grooming	

Colours and patterns
Brown spotted tabby only.

Like the mountain bobcat from which it derives its name, the Pixiebob has a thick coat, tufted ears, a pointed face, and a powerful body, and moves with loose-limbed grace. A common feature of this breed – which, unusually, is accepted in the breed standard – is the occurrence of extra toes (polydactylism) on one or more paws. Both the Pixiebob shorthair and a longhaired variant (pp.190–1) have richly coloured, spotted coats that complete the illusion of a wild cat. Despite appearances, the Pixiebob is entirely domestic in character, loves family life, clings to its owners, plays with children, and good-naturedly accepts other pets.

Thickly furred above eyes

Brick-red nose leather

Short coat has woolly texture and stands away from body

Brown spotted tabby coat

Deep flanks

Well-muscled body

Short bob tail

Lighter colour on underparts, throat, and chest

Broad chest

Long, heavily boned legs

Long, broad paws

AMERICAN RINGTAIL

A WELL-BUILT AND PLUSH-COATED CAT WITH A TWIST IN ITS TAIL

Place of origin USA

Date of origin 1990s

Breed registries CFA, TICA

Weight range 3–7kg (7–15lb)

Grooming

Colours and patterns
All colours, shades, and patterns.

No other cat possesses this breed's unique tail, which is carried in a flexible curl over the back or flank. The American Ringtail was discovered by chance in California and, so far, its development has included the introduction of Oriental-type lines. These cats are still few and far between, but interest among breeders is gradually increasing. There is also a longhaired version. Ringtails love games, climbing, and nosing around anything that appeals to their strong sense of curiosity. The soft trilling sounds that they make gave them their original name of Ringtail Sing-a-Ling.

Large almond-shaped eyes

Soft, dense brown classic tabby coat with plush texture

Flexible tail carried in a ring over back

Long body with athletic build

Broad, wedge-shaped head

Ears deeply cupped

Powerful hindquarters

Medium-length, square muzzle

Hindlegs slightly longer than forelegs

White markings on chest and chin

Large, oval white paws

Very large, broad-based, upright ears

Body has fine "peach fuzz", black tortie and white coat

Prominent cheekbones

Muscular, rounded rump

Well-rounded belly

Thick paw pads

Wrinkled skin around head and shoulders

Slightly arched neck

Pronounced whisker pads lack whiskers

Whip-like tail tapers to fine point

SPHYNX

THIS HAIRLESS CAT HAS AN ENDEARINGLY IMPISH CHARACTER

Place of origin	Canada
Date of origin	1960s
Breed registries	CFA, FIFe, GCCF, TICA
Weight range	3.5–7kg (8–15lb)

Grooming

Colours and patterns
All colours, shades, and patterns.

Probably the best known of the hairless cats that have appeared around the world, the Sphynx originated in Canada, and was named for its supposed resemblance to the Ancient Egyptian sculpture of the mythical Sphinx. The cat's hairlessness is a natural mutation, and interest in its development dates from the birth of a hairless male kitten produced by a short-coated farm cat in Ontario in 1966. This kitten, along with other hairless kittens that appeared over the following decade, was used to found the breed.

Although hairlessness is commonly accompanied by other mutations, careful selective breeding, including outcrosses to Devon Rex (pp.128–9) and Cornish Rex (pp.126–7) cats, has ensured that the Sphynx is relatively free of genetic problems. Sphynx cats are not completely bald – most have a coating of fine, suede-like fuzz on their bodies and often a little thin hair on their head, tail, and paws. Undeniably an extraordinary looking cat, with its enormous

ears, wrinkled skin, and rounded belly, the Sphynx does not appeal to everyone but its delightfully sociable and loving nature has made more than a few converts. It is easy to live with but needs to be kept indoors and protected from temperature extremes. Lack of a normal coat also means that excess body oils cannot be absorbed, so regular washing is required. Cats used to baths from an early age are unlikely to object.

WRINKLY SKIN

The Sphynx's wrinkled skin is not unique to the breed – all cats are the same under their fur. Sphynx kittens are wrinkly all over; adults have wrinkles mainly on the shoulders and head.

DONSKOY

A CAT WITH OTHERWORLDLY LOOKS BUT A LOVABLE NATURE

Place of origin	Russia
Date of origin	1980s
Breed registries	FIFe, TICA
Weight range	3.5–7kg (8–15lb)

Grooming

Colours and patterns
All colours, shades, and patterns.

The founder of this breed (also known as the Don Sphynx) was an ill-treated kitten rescued from the streets in the Russian city of Rostov-on-Don. This stray lost its apparently normal coat as it matured, and produced offspring with the same mutation. Various coat types occur in the Donskoy – some individuals are truly hairless while others have a partial coat that can be fuzzy or even wavy. Uniquely, the hairless types may develop temporary fur patches in winter. With wrinkled skin and outsize ears, the Donskoy does not have universal appeal, but aficionados praise its gentleness, sparkling personality, and social ease. Grooming consists of regular bathing to remove excess oil from the skin.

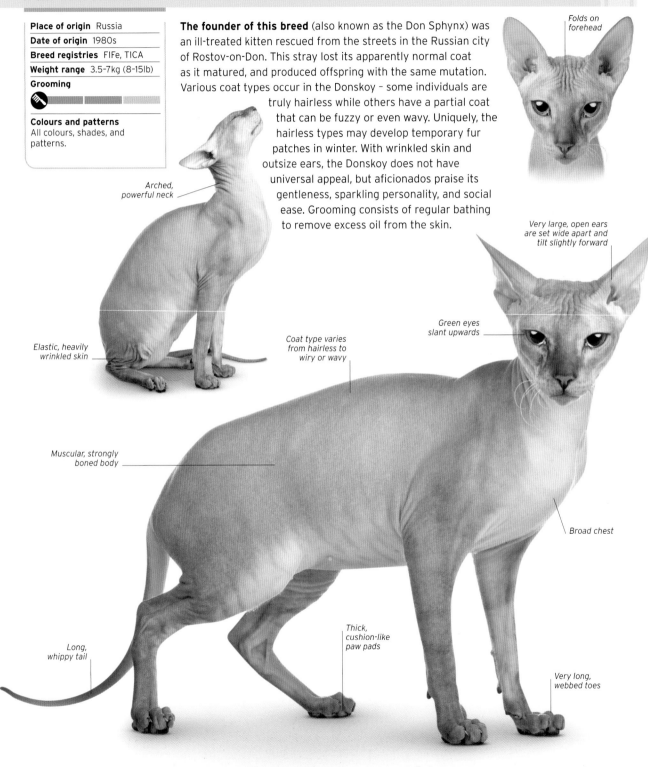

Folds on forehead

Arched, powerful neck

Very large, open ears are set wide apart and tilt slightly forward

Green eyes slant upwards

Elastic, heavily wrinkled skin

Coat type varies from hairless to wiry or wavy

Muscular, strongly boned body

Broad chest

Long, whippy tail

Thick, cushion-like paw pads

Very long, webbed toes

PETERBALD

AN ELEGANT, GRACEFUL BREED WITH A VARIETY OF COAT TYPES

Place of origin Russia

Date of origin 1990s

Breed registries FIFe, TICA

Weight range 3.5–7kg (8–15lb)

Grooming

Colours and patterns
All colours, shades, and patterns.

Originating in Russia, the Peterbald is a fairly new breed created by crossing the Oriental Shorthair (pp.43–51) with the Donskoy (left). This cat is highly variable, and may be completely hairless, covered with a fine soft down, or possess a dense, stiff coat with a brush-like texture. Kittens born with a coat may become hairless as they mature, sometimes retaining downy-coated points. The Peterbald has a pleasant temperament and makes a good family cat. Hairless or very thin-coated varieties need protection from the elements and are probably best kept indoors. The skin of hairless types may have a sticky feel and needs regular bathing.

Blunt muzzle

Firm, graceful body

Long, fine-boned legs

Long, triangular head with high cheekbones

Huge, flared ears with broad bases

Straight nose runs from flat forehead

Whiskers kinked and broken

Long, whippy tail

Oval paws with long, flexible toes

URAL REX

THIS UNUSUAL-LOOKING REX BREED IS NOT YET WIDELY KNOWN

Place of origin	Russia
Date of origin	1980s
Breed registries	Other
Weight range	3.5-7kg (8-15lb)

Grooming

Colours and patterns
Various colours and patterns, including tabby.

The first of these wavy-coated cats was born near Yekaterinburg, a major Russian city set in the foothills of the Ural Mountains. Carefully developed over three decades, the Ural Rex is very popular among cat fanciers in Russia and is also now being bred in Germany. This breed's fine, dense, double coat may be short or semi-long; the distinctive, close-lying waves, which have an elastic quality, can take up to two years to develop fully. Grooming is not difficult but must be carried out regularly. The Ural Rex is described as a quiet and good-natured cat that makes an excellent household companion.

Upright ears set high on head

Prominent cheekbones

Large, oval eyes set wide apart

Slim, muscular, relatively short body

Broad, flat forehead

Short, wedge-shaped head

Fine, silky black-smoke coat lies close to body in loose curls

White chest, underparts, and legs

Medium-length, moderately thin tail

Slender legs with small paws

LAPERM

A BRIGHT AND INQUISITIVE CAT WITH A KITTENISH ENERGY THAT LASTS INTO ADULTHOOD

Place of origin USA

Date of origin 1980s

Breed registries CFA, GCCF, TICA

Weight range 3.5-5.5kg (8-12lb)

Grooming

Colours and patterns
All colours, shades, and patterns, including colourpoint.

This rex-coated breed originated on a farm in Oregon, USA, and was later developed into both shorthaired and longhaired (pp.196-7) versions. The LaPerm has a highly strokable coat that may be either wavy or curly and has a light, springy texture. Outgoing and not shy about asking for attention, this cat makes a loving and lively pet. LaPerms adapt themselves easily to homes of all types and become deeply attached to their owners. They need company and should not be left alone for too long. Gentle combing or the occasional shampoo and towel dry are recommended as the best ways of maintaining the coat.

Large, expressive gold eyes

Very long, wavy whiskers

Slightly rounded, wedge-shaped head

Kittens

Medium-long, well-muscled body

Tabby pattern evident on head

Long, broad nose

Firm chin

Curly, standaway red tabby coat has springy texture

Red tabby pattern masked by curly coat

Rounded paws

Rectangular, well-muscled body

Plush, curly black and white coat

Broad-based, wide-set ears

Large eyes with sweet expression

Round, smooth skull

Curly, brittle whiskers

Short, square muzzle

Medium-long, well-boned legs

Large, round paws

Curls lie flat against tail

SELKIRK REX

A HAPPY "TEDDY BEAR" OF A CAT THAT ENJOYS A LOT OF COMPANY

Place of origin	USA
Date of origin	1980s
Breed registries	CFA, TICA
Weight range	3–5kg (7–11lb)

Grooming

Colours and patterns
All colours, shades, and patterns.

This cat takes its name from the Selkirk Mountains near its place of origin in Montana, USA. Created in the late 1980s, the breed had its beginnings in an animal rescue centre, where a curly-coated kitten appeared among an otherwise straight-coated litter born to a feral cat. This kitten became the founding female of the Selkirk Rex. As the breed was developed, planned matings with pedigree cats produced both the Selkirk Rex shorthair and a longer-coated type (p.194) that was the result of crosses with Persians. Straight-coated variants are common in litters of both types.

The dense, soft coat of the Selkirk Rex falls into random curls or waves, rather than in the neat lines sometimes seen in other rex breeds. A greater degree of curl often occurs around the neck and belly. The whiskers are sparse and curly, and tend to snap off easily.

Grooming a Selkirk Rex is not difficult but a light touch is advisable, as over-vigorous brushing can flatten out the curls.

Though calm and tolerant, this cat is far from staid and loves a hug. Selkirks stay kittenish for years and always enjoy games.

GOING CURLY

The curls of a Selkirk Rex can take up to two years to develop fully. Kittens are born with curly coats that usually straighten out for a few months before starting to turn curly again when the cat is about eight months old.

GROWING A FULL COAT
All Cornish Rex kittens are born with wavy coats, but some of them lose this for a few weeks and have a temporary, suede-like covering. By three months, the waves should be nearly fully formed.

CORNISH REX

THIS ATHLETIC CAT HAS CURLS FROM WHISKERS TO TAIL

Place of origin	UK
Date of origin	1950s
Breed registries	CFA, FIFe, GCCF, TICA
Weight range	2.5–4kg (6–9lb)

Grooming

Colours and patterns
All self and shaded colours and patterns, including tabby, tortie, colourpoint, and bicolour.

The founder of this svelte breed was a wavy-coated male cat born in a Cornish farmhouse. Descendants of this original sire were crossed with other breeds – including the Siamese (pp.54–7), Russian Blue (p.66), and American (p.61) and British Shorthairs (pp.68–77) – improving the stamina and genetic diversity of the Cornish Rex, and adding a wide variety of colours. With its super-fine, rippled coat and streamlined body, this cat stands out from all the rest. It is an extrovert with a large repertoire of amusing antics and a kittenish outlook on life, but turns into an affectionate lap cat when play is over. Because of its thin coat, this breed is vulnerable to temperature extremes and should be groomed with a light touch. In the USA it has developed differently and has a more wedge-shaped head.

Large, oval eyes are set wide apart

High, chiselled cheekbones

Slim, elongated, well-muscled body

Outer ear is hairless

Fairly small, wedge-shaped head

Straight nose

Short, fine, white coat forms tight, uniform waves

Finely boned, long, slender legs

Small, oval paws

Exceptionally
large ears, very
wide at base

Nose has
distinct stop

Comparatively
small head set
on long neck

Wide
cheekbones

Firm, muscular,
body

Short muzzle
with curly
whiskers

Fine, curly
silver tabby
coat has few
guard hairs

Long, slender
legs with small,
oval paws

Long,
tapering tail

DEVON REX

NICKNAMED THE "PIXIE CAT", THIS MISCHIEVOUS BREED HAS AN ABUNDANCE OF ENERGY

Place of origin	UK
Date of origin	1960s
Breed registries	CFA, FIFe, GCCF, TICA
Weight range	2.5–4kg (6–9lb)

Grooming

Colours and patterns
All colours, shades,
and patterns.

A curly-coated feral tom and an adopted stray tortoiseshell were the founders of this highly specialized breed, which originated in Buckfastleigh, Devon. A litter produced by this unlikely pair included a curly-coated kitten, which was used in the first programme to develop the breed. To begin with, it was assumed that this new Devonian line could be crossed with the Cornish Rex (p.127), another wavy-coated breed discovered a short distance away and a few years earlier. When only normal-coated kittens resulted from the matings, it was realized that two different recessive genes, arising in surprisingly close geographical proximity, had produced slightly different rexed coats.

The coat of the Devon Rex is fine and very short, with few guard hairs. Ideally, the waves should be loose and distributed evenly over the body, but the degree of wave or curl varies from cat to cat and may alter with seasonal shedding of hair or as a cat matures. The whiskers are crinkly and tend to be brittle, breaking off before reaching full length. Because of their thin coats, these cats can seem warmer to the touch than most breeds, but they easily become chilled and need draught-proof accommodation. A Devon Rex's coat usually needs little more than a wipe-down to keep it in good condition; these cats will also tolerate gentle bathing, provided they are introduced to water when they are young kittens.

Despite its slender, leggy appearance, the Devon Rex is far from fragile, and possesses boundless energy for playing games and scaling heights. This cat adores attention and is not suitable for a family that will be away from the home all day.

GERMAN REX

A CAT THAT NEEDS PLENTY OF "QUALITY TIME" WITH ITS HUMAN FAMILY

Place of origin	Germany
Date of origin	1940s
Breed registries	FIFe
Weight range	2.5-4.5kg (6-10lb)

Grooming

Colours and patterns
All colours, shades, and patterns.

A feral cat adopted in Berlin just after the end of World War II was the founding female of this breed. As the German Rex was developed, cats were imported to other parts of Europe and to the USA. The wavy coat of this cat arises through the same mutant gene that appears in the Cornish Rex (p.127), which for some years was included in German Rex breeding programmes; in some countries the two breeds are not recognized as separate. A good-natured and friendly cat, the German Rex will play with anyone but also likes quiet times staying close to its owners. As the short coat does not absorb natural oils efficiently, regular bathing is necessary.

Brilliant blue eyes

Short, curly whiskers

Rounded paws

Short, wavy coat with velvety texture

Kittens

Broad-based ears

Round head with well-defined cheekbones

Cream coat shaded with sepia in places

Medium-length, strongly built body

Sepia pointing on tail, legs, and face

Strong, rounded chest

Medium-length, moderately fine legs

AMERICAN WIREHAIR

THIS VERSATILE, FRIENDLY CAT IS HAPPY INDOORS OR OUTDOORS AND WITH FAMILIES OF ALL AGES

Place of origin	USA
Date of origin	1960s
Breed registries	CFA, TICA
Weight range	3.5–7kg (8–15lb)

Grooming

Colours and patterns
Variety of self colours and shades in various patterns, including bicolour, tabby, and tortie.

In New York State, in 1966, a wire-haired kitten appeared in a litter born to two domestic cats with normal coats. This was the founder of the American Wirehair breed, which was later developed by using American Shorthairs (p.61). The genetic mutation that produced the distinctive coat is not known to have occurred anywhere outside the USA. In a Wirehair, each hair is crimped and bends over or forms a hook at the end, resulting in a harsh, springy texture that has been likened to wire wool. In some cats the coat can be brittle, so grooming – preferably by bathing – should be gentle to avoid damage.

Large, round copper-coloured eyes

Curly whiskers

Prominent cheekbones

Dense, springy brown classic tabby and white coat with crimped hairs and coarse texture

Rounded rump

Medium to large, well-muscled body

Back level from shoulders to rump

Medium-size ears with rounded tips

Medium-boned, muscular legs

Firm, rounded paws

HOUSECAT – SHORTHAIR
THESE HARDY CATS MAKE EXCELLENT, EASY-TO-KEEP PETS

The first domestic cats had short coats, and the type still predominates wherever in the world cats are kept as house pets. Random-bred shorthairs occur in nearly every possible colour permutation, with tabbies, torties, and traditional self colours being the most common. The majority of these cats are solidly in the middle range when it comes to body shape. Selective breeding, which has created some extreme lines, has largely bypassed the shorthaired housecat, although occasionally a hint of, for example, the lean Oriental shape suggests an out-of-the-ordinary parentage.

Typical tabby "M" marking on forehead

RED CLASSIC TABBY AND WHITE
Large size and a dense coat could point to British or American Shorthair in the history of this handsome cat. However, his green eyes may be part of a different inheritance.

BLUE AND WHITE
In housecats white markings are rarely as symmetrical as those considered desirable in pedigrees. However, a solid colour splashed with white is always striking, and a random effect adds individual charm.

Irregularly spaced ring markings on tail

BROWN TABBY
The broken stripes on this cat are, in fact, intermediate between mackerel and spotted tabby patterns. Tabby markings often occur in domestic cats and show up well on short coats.

Black and red markings intermingled

TORTIE AND WHITE
Tortoiseshell, or tortie, patterning occurs in many colour forms, black and red being the traditional combination. A tortie with white areas over more than half its body is known as a calico cat in the USA.

BLUE MACKEREL TABBY AND WHITE
While tabbies with white markings are very common, the blue variation would be a lucky find in a random-bred cat. This one's markings are indistinct against the background colour.

RAGDOLL
One of the largest pedigree cats, the semi-longhaired Ragdoll was developed in the 1960s. This spectacular breed comes in several dramatic patterns, all with bright blue eyes.

LONGHAIRS

It is thought that long hair in domestic cats arose as a natural genetic mutation, most likely in response to cold climates. Where this advantageous gene was passed on among cats living in isolated areas, such as mountain regions, longhaired populations would have arisen. Wild cats with long coats are a rarity and have no role in the ancestry of domestic longhairs.

The curly-coated Selkirk Rex longhair is an unusual variation

Types of longhair

The first longhaired cats seen in Western Europe arrived some time in the 16th century. These were the Angoras, a slender, silky-coated Turkish breed that enjoyed a certain popularity until they were usurped by a new type of longhair, the Persian, in the 19th century. Sturdier than the Angoras, Persians had longer, thicker fur, immense tails, and round faces. By the end of the 19th century they were the longhair of choice for cat lovers. The Angora vanished, not to be seen again until the breed was re-created by enthusiasts in the 1960s (p.159).

The Persian remains a steady favourite, but since the 20th century other longhairs have been attracting attention. These include cats described as semi-longhaired, which have medium-long coats but a less dense, fluffy undercoat than the Persian. One of the most magnificent of the semi-longhairs is the Maine Coon,

native to North America. Huge and handsome, this breed has a shaggy look due to the variable length of the hairs in its topcoat. Almost equally striking is the big blue-eyed Ragdoll, while the brush-tailed Somali has the graceful lines of the Abyssinian cat from which it was developed. More in the style of the original Angoras is the beautiful Balinese – a semi-longhair version of the Siamese – which has silky, flowing, close-lying fur.

Striving for yet more variety, breeders have crossed longhairs with some of the more unusual shorthairs. Bobtails, curled-ear and folded-ear breeds, the wavy-coated Selkirk Rex, and the LaPerm with its fleece-like curly fur are all now found with luxuriantly long coats.

Grooming longhairs

Many longhaired cats shed their coats heavily, especially in the warmer seasons, when they can have a much sleeker

appearance. Frequent grooming – a daily session may be needed in some breeds – keeps loose hairs to a minimum and prevents the thick undercoat from matting.

MAINE COON
This American breed was once an outdoor farm cat. Its naturally thick coat gave protection in bitter New England winters.

PERSIAN
For more than a hundred years the extravagantly coated Persian has been the most popular longhair.

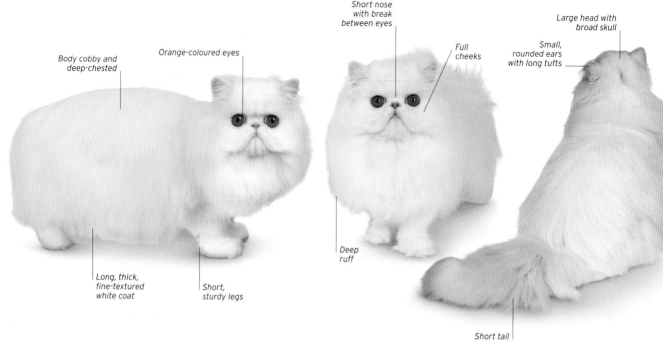

Body cobby and deep-chested

Orange-coloured eyes

Short nose with break between eyes

Full cheeks

Large head with broad skull

Small, rounded ears with long tufts

Long, thick, fine-textured white coat

Short, sturdy legs

Deep ruff

Short tail

PERSIAN - SELF

THIS CHARMING CAT IS THE ORIGINAL VERSION OF THE WORLD'S FAVOURITE LONGHAIR

Place of origin	UK
Date of origin	1800s
Breed registries	CFA, FIFe, GCCF, TICA
Weight range	3.5–7kg (8–15lb)

Grooming

Colours and patterns
Black, white, blue, red, cream, chocolate, and lilac.

By the end of the 19th century, when pedigree cat shows were starting to attract worldwide interest, the Persian (sometimes referred to as the Longhair) was already very popular in the UK and the USA. This luxuriously coated cat came to the show benches after a long but obscure history in Europe, and it is not known whether the true ancestors of the breed did, in fact, originate in Persia (Iran). The first recognized Persians were self-coloured, that is, they had coats in one solid colour throughout.

The earliest known examples of the breed were pure white, often with blue eyes – a colour combination commonly associated with deafness unless breeding is carefully managed. Cross-breeding with self Persians in other colours produced orange eyes, and white Persians with orange, blue, or odd-coloured eyes (one of each colour) became accepted. Queen Victoria can be given credit for making blue Persians popular – they were her favourite cats – and

black and red were other early self colours. Since about the 1920s onwards, further self varieties have been developed, including cream, chocolate, and lilac.

Characteristically, a Persian has a round head with a flat face, snub nose, and large, round, appealing eyes. The body is compact and sturdily built, and the legs are short and strong. The magnificently thick, long coat is a major commitment for the owner of a Persian. Daily grooming is a must to prevent the fur from tangling or developing impenetrable mats that are hard to remove.

Persians are renowned for their gentle, affectionate temperament and home-loving personality. These are definitely not all-action cats, although they can be charmingly playful if offered a toy.

The flattened features of the Persian, over-emphasized in modern breeding programmes, have led to health issues. Breathing difficulties and problems with the tear ducts are common in this cat.

PERSIAN – BLUE- AND ODD-EYED BICOLOUR

THESE UNCOMMON PERSIANS ARE HARD TO FIND BUT THEIR POPULARITY IS ON THE RISE

Place of origin UK

Date of origin 1800s

Breed registries CFA, FIFe, GCCF, TICA

Weight range 3.5–7kg (8–15lb)

Grooming

Colours and patterns
White with various self colours, including black, red, blue, cream, chocolate, and lilac.

Accepted in the cat fancy world only since the late 1990s, the Blue- and Odd-eyed Bicolour and Tricolour are variations of the Persian Bicolour (p.154). The Odd-eyed is less common than the Blue-eyed, although its enchantingly different look is increasing in popularity. In this cat one eye is blue and the other copper, with both eyes equally brilliant in colour. The mismatch is difficult to produce, as a mating between two odd-eyed cats does not guarantee a litter of odd-eyed kittens.

One eye is blue, the other copper

Red "van" pattern (coloration on head and tail only)

Level back

White inner ear tufts

Great breadth between ears

Snub nose

Deep ruff

Short auburn-coloured tail

Full cheeks

Pure white fur stands out from body

Round paws with long toe tufts

PERSIAN - CAMEO

THIS BREED HAS SOFTLY BLENDED COLOURS IN A RIPPLING COAT

Place of origin USA, Australia, and New Zealand

Date of origin 1950s

Breed registries CFA, FIFe, GCCF, TICA

Weight range 3.5–7kg (8–15lb)

Grooming

Colours and patterns
Red, cream, black, blue, lilac, and chocolate self colours and tortie patterns.

Regarded by many cat fanciers as the most glamorous of all the Persian colours, this version was developed in the 1950s by crossing Smoke (p.148) and Tortoiseshell (p.152) Persians. The fur of a Cameo is white with colour carried at the ends of the hair shafts to varying degrees. In the "tipped" variety the colour appears only at the very tip of each hair, but extends to up to one-third of the hair shaft in "shaded" cats. Cameo gives the effect, especially as the cat moves, of a coat rippling with changing hues.

Deep copper eyes

Pink nose leather

Cream shaded cameo coat

Shading on legs

Pale inner ear tufts

Darker markings on face

Main area of colour on back and flanks

Ears set towards side of head

Underside of plumed tail lighter in colour

Paler fur on chest and underparts

Hair shorter on lower legs

PERSIAN - CHINCHILLA

THIS SILVERY-COATED BREED HAS MOVIE-STAR LOOKS

Place of origin	UK
Date of origin	1880s
Breed registries	CFA, FIFe, GCCF, TICA
Weight range	3.5-7kg (8-15lb)

Grooming

Colours and patterns
White, tipped with black.

The first Chinchilla appeared in the 1880s, but it was the "James Bond" series of films, starting in the 1960s, that brought this cat fame when it was seen on screen as the pet of the super-spy's arch enemy, Blofeld. Chinchillas have a shimmering, silvery-white coat in which each hair is tipped with black. The breed's name derives from the likeness of its coat coloration to that of a small South American rodent called the chinchilla, once a victim of the fashion trade for its beautiful, soft fur.

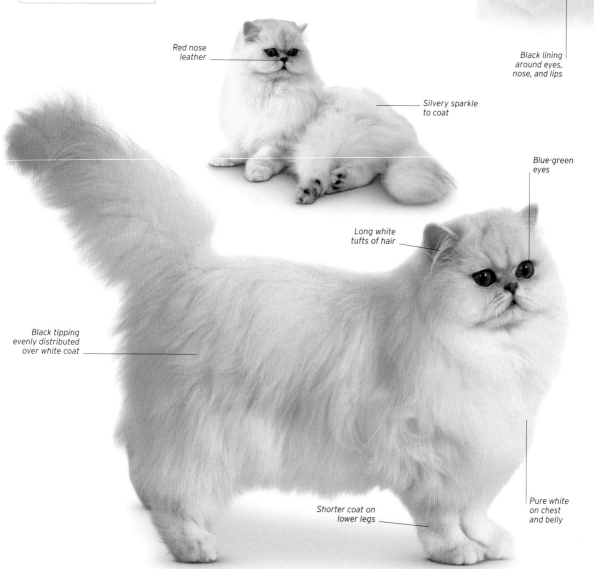

Black lining around eyes, nose, and lips

Red nose leather

Silvery sparkle to coat

Blue-green eyes

Long white tufts of hair

Black tipping evenly distributed over white coat

Shorter coat on lower legs

Pure white on chest and belly

PERSIAN - GOLDEN

ONCE REGARDED AS THE "WRONG" COLOUR, THIS CAT IS NOW A MUCH-PRIZED PET

Place of origin	UK
Date of origin	1920s
Breed registries	CFA, FIFe, GCCF, TICA
Weight range	3.5-7kg (8-15lb)

Grooming

Colours and patterns
Apricot to golden with seal-brown or black tipping.

Recognized as a new breed in the USA since the 1970s, this cat has a gloriously coloured coat of rich apricot to golden fur that is widely admired. Yet the first Golden Persians, which appeared in the 1920s in litters born to Chinchillas (opposite), were regarded as rejects as far as the pedigree cat world was concerned. They were known generally as "brownies" and, though barred from the show bench, made appealing pets. Later, breeders saw the potential of Goldens and worked to develop this lovely Persian variation.

Blue-green eyes

Rose-pink nose leather

Domed head

Eyes, lips, and nose rimmed with black

Thick ruff around neck

Kitten

Lightest colouring on chest and belly

Long pale apricot tufts of hair

Golden coat with rich colouring on back

Paler underside to tail

Darker coloration on legs due to seal-brown tipping

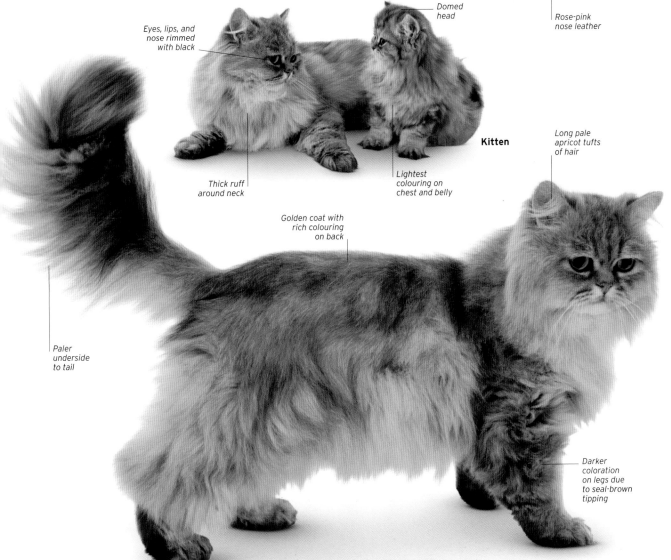

PERSIAN - PEWTER

THIS STRIKING, COPPER-EYED CAT HAS AN ATTRACTIVELY TIPPED COAT

Place of origin UK

Date of origin 1900s

Breed registries CFA, FIFe, GCCF, TICA

Weight range 3.5–7kg (8–15lb)

Grooming

Colours and patterns
Very pale with black or blue tipping.

Years of careful breeding, at first using crosses with Persian Chinchillas (p.140), produced the two current variations of Pewter. These cats, originally referred to as Blue Chinchillas, have pale, almost white, coats with blue- or black-tipped hairs. This coloration gives the effect of a mantle extending from the top of the head and down the back. Pewter kittens are born with traditional tabby markings, which gradually fade in intensity but are still retained to some degree in adult cats. The very special look of this breed is enhanced by its characteristic deep orange to copper-coloured eyes.

Nose break between eyes

Dark-rimmed, copper-coloured eyes

Darkest tipping on back and flanks

Ghost tabby "M" marking on forehead

Very pale chest

Black pewter coat

Dark tip to tail

Faint tabby markings on legs

Face lightly tipped only

PERSIAN - CAMEO BICOLOUR

THIS LOVELY BREED IS TRULY A PERSIAN OF MANY COLOURS

Place of origin USA, New Zealand, and Australia

Date of origin 1950s

Breed registries CFA, FIFe, GCCF, TICA

Weight range 3.5–7kg (8–15lb)

Grooming

Colours and patterns
Red, cream, blue-cream, black, blue, lilac, and chocolate colours with white; tortie pattern with white.

The colour combinations of this version of the Cameo (p.139) are almost endless. As well as the shading and tipping that characterize the Cameo coat, in which the hair shafts are coloured only part way along their length, the addition of both bicolour and tricolour patterns make this breed seem like many different cats. Shades of red are common, but black, blue, chocolate, cream, and tortoiseshell (black and red, or blue and cream) also appear, all with extensive areas of white. The contrast between the patches of sparkling white and colour of varying intensity is stunning.

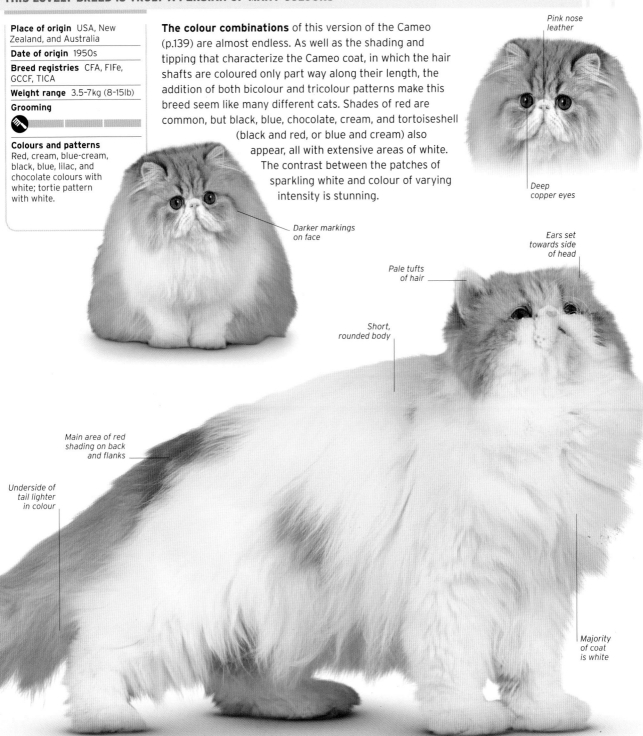

Pink nose leather

Deep copper eyes

Darker markings on face

Ears set towards side of head

Pale tufts of hair

Short, rounded body

Main area of red shading on back and flanks

Underside of tail lighter in colour

Majority of coat is white

PERSIAN - SHADED SILVER

AN EXQUISITELY COLOURED CAT WITH LUMINOUS BLUE-GREEN EYES

Place of origin	UK
Date of origin	1800s
Breed registries	CFA, FIFe, GCCF, TICA
Weight range	3.5-7kg (8-15lb)

Grooming

Colours and patterns
White with black tipping.

This Persian bears some resemblance to the Chinchilla (p.140), both breeds having white coats tipped on the ends of the hairs with a darker colour. At one time, these cats were described as "silvers". However, over decades of development from the 20th century onwards, Chinchillas have become paler and the Shaded Silver can now usually be distinguished by having the darker colouring of the two. In particular, breeders of Shaded Silvers strive to achieve the characteristic dark mantle that falls over the back.

Blue-green eyes

Eyes, nose, and lips are black-rimmed

Silver shaded coat

Rose-pink nose leather

White fur on chin and chest

Well-developed nose stop

White underside to tail

Mantle of black tipping, darkest on back, flanks, and tail

Short, sturdy legs

PERSIAN – SILVER TABBY

THIS CAT IS A SILKY, SILVERY-COATED VERSION OF THE TRADITIONAL TABBY

Place of origin	UK
Date of origin	1800s
Breed registries	CFA, FIFe, GCCF, TICA
Weight range	3.5–7kg (8–15lb)
Grooming	

Colours and patterns
Silver tabby; tortie silver tabby; all with white patches.

Some of the most delicately coloured Persians of all are the Silver Tabbies. These cats have well-defined tabby coat patterns, but the warm coppery ground colours of the traditional tabby are replaced by a silvery- or bluish-white undercoat. Bicolour Silver Tabby cats have clear white areas, preferably as a minimum on the muzzle, chest, underparts, and sometimes legs. In the Tricolours a further colour, such as a shade of red or brown, is blended into the coat.

Large green eyes

Pink nose leather

Deep white neck ruff extends to chest

Well-tufted toes

Distinct "M" marking on forehead

Long white tufts of hair

Silvery-white undercoat

Dark tabby markings on body

Short and bushy tail

Barring evident on legs

PERSIAN - SMOKE

THIS RARE-COLOURED BREED HAS BEEN SAVED FROM THE BRINK OF EXTINCTION

Place of origin UK

Date of origin 1860s

Breed registries CFA, FIFe, GCCF, TICA

Weight range 3.5-7kg (8-15lb)

Grooming

Colours and patterns
White deeply tipped with colour, including black, blue, cream, and red, and in tortie patterns.

In the coat patterning of the Smoke, each hair is pale at the base, becoming darker by degrees along its length. Smoke kittens are born without any apparent sign of this colouring, which does not start developing until the cat is several months old. Smoke Persians were recorded as early as the 1860s but they have never been common. By the 1940s this breed had all but disappeared. Fortunately, a few enthusiasts continued to develop the Smoke, creating new interest in the breed and extending its range of colours.

Dark blue mask and ears

Black nose leather

Full white frill on black smoke coat

Typical cobby Persian body

Legs are solid colour

Short, bushy tail

Blue smoke coat

Ears set far apart

White undercoat, more apparent in motion

Lighter underparts

PERSIAN – SMOKE BICOLOUR

BEAUTIFULLY BLENDED COLOURS MAKE THIS CAT ONE OF THE PRETTIEST PERSIANS

Place of origin UK

Date of origin 1900s

Breed registries CFA, FIFe, GCCF, FICA

Weight range 3.5–7kg (8–15lb)

Grooming

Colours and patterns
White with smoke colours, including blue, black, red, chocolate, lilac, and various tortoiseshells.

This multi-hued breed has a coat combining areas of white with various smoke colours, in which each hair is coloured for most of its length but is white at the base. Smoke produces greater depth of colour than in shaded or tipped coats, and the pale base may not be apparent until the cat moves. Bicoloured Smoke Persians can have areas of black, blue, chocolate, lilac, and red smoke with white, while the Tricolours include several tortoiseshell smokes, such as blue and cream tortie.

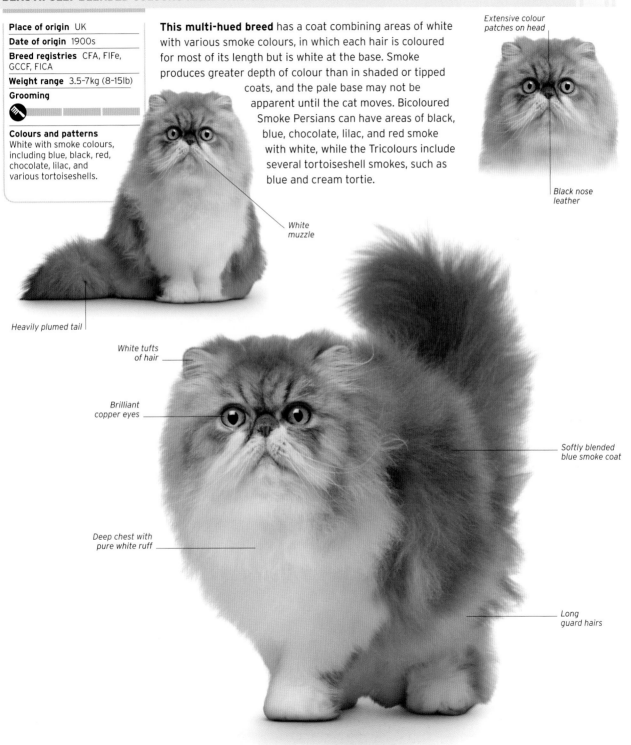

Extensive colour patches on head

Black nose leather

White muzzle

Heavily plumed tail

White tufts of hair

Brilliant copper eyes

Softly blended blue smoke coat

Deep chest with pure white ruff

Long guard hairs

PERSIAN – TABBY AND TORTIE – TABBY

THIS GENTLE CAT HAS BEEN BRED IN A RICH VARIETY OF COLOURS AND PATTERNS

Place of origin UK

Date of origin 1800s

Breed registries CFA, FIFe, GCCF, TICA

Weight range 3.5–7kg (8–15lb)

Grooming

Colours and patterns
Many colours also with silver tipping in tabby and tortie-tabby patterns.

The tabbies have a longer history than many of the other Persians. Brown tabbies appeared in some of the earliest cat shows in the UK in the 1870s, and one of the first purebred cat fancy clubs was established to promote the breed. Since those days, the Persian Tabby has been developed in several colours, and three pattern types are accepted: classic (or blotched), mackerel (with narrow streaks), and spotted. In Tortie-Tabbies (sometimes known as patched tabbies) the tabby markings overlay a bicoloured ground coat.

Red nose leather

Black line runs from corner of eye

Round copper-coloured eyes

Nose has sharp break between eyes

Brown classic tabby coat

Barring on legs

Dense black markings on body

Tabby "M" mark on forehead

Full, brush-like tail

Short, sturdy legs with large, round paws

Necklace markings on upper chest

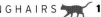

PERSIAN - TABBY BICOLOUR
A BREED WITH RICH TABBY COLOURING HIGHLIGHTED BY WHITE PATCHES

Place of origin UK

Date of origin Post 1900

Breed registries CFA, FIFE, GCCF, TICA

Weight range 3.5–7kg (8–15lb)

Grooming

Colours and patterns
Classic and mackerel tabby pattern, in various colours with white.

This lovely variation of the Persian combines sparkling white with the warm colours of the tabby. Two types of markings are accepted: classic tabby (sometimes called blotched tabby), in which the markings appear as large, smudged areas; and mackerel tabby, which is marked with thinner dark streaks or stripes. Tabby Bicolour and Tricolour Persians were first given championship status in the 1980s, and their beautiful markings, softly blurred by the lush coat, have made them firm favourites with cat breeders and owners.

Pink nose leather

Brilliant copper eyes

White muzzle and chest

White mittens on paws

Full dark-coloured tail

Shorter hair on forehead and face

Small, rounded ears

Tricolour with soft classic tabby markings

Body set low on legs

PERSIAN – TORTIE AND TORTIE & WHITE

THESE PERSIANS WITH POPULAR COLOURS ARE NOT ALWAYS EASY TO OBTAIN

Place of origin UK

Date of origin 1880s

Breed registries CFA, FIFe, GCCF, TICA

Weight range 3.5–7kg (8–15lb)

Grooming

Colours and patterns
Tortoiseshell (black and red), chocolate tortoiseshell, lilac-cream, and blue-cream; also with white patches.

Tortoiseshell cats – frequently called torties – have a coat that is a mixture of two colours, giving a mottled appearance. Persian Torties have been known since the late 19th century, but they have always been difficult to breed consistently. Their genetic make-up means that nearly all cats with tortie colouring are females and the few males that do occur are sterile. There is a tricoloured version of this Persian, the Tortie and White (known as Calico in the USA).

Bright copper eyes

Black nose leather

Fine-textured, silky tortie and white coat

Clear black and red patches on body

Very short muzzle

White chest and muzzle

White legs and paws

Several shades of red blend softly with black areas in tortie coat

Long tufts of red hair

Strong, thick legs

PAINTBOX PATTERN
A splash of red tabby added to black and white creates a vivid mix of colours. Tortie and white (also known as calico) is particularly dramatic when seen on the long, silky hair of a Persian.

PERSIAN - BICOLOUR

A LONGHAIR WITH BOLD COLOUR PATCHES FOR EXTRA GLAMOUR

Place of origin	UK
Date of origin	1800s
Breed registries	CFA, FIFe, GCCF, TICA
Weight range	3.5–7kg (8–15lb)

Grooming

Colours and patterns
White with various self colours, including black, red, blue, cream, chocolate, and lilac, and with tortie patterns.

Up until the 1960s bicoloured Persians were of little interest to breeders, and were considered suitable only as pets. Today, they are challenging the self colours in popularity on the show benches. One of the first bicolours to be recognized was black and white, once referred to as "magpie"; now many other solid colours combined with white are accepted. In producing bicolour and tortie and white cats, breeders aim for clearly defined, symmetrical markings – an ideal that is difficult to achieve.

Chocolate colour on head

White muzzle

Black nose leather

Colour patches well defined and symmetrical

Long hair at base of ears

Copper-coloured eyes

Chocolate and white, fine-haired, silky coat

Chocolate-coloured tail

White chest and underside

White legs and paws

PERSIAN – COLOURPOINT

THIS CAT HAS SHOW-STOPPING LOOKS AND A PEACEFUL TEMPERAMENT

Place of origin USA

Date of origin 1930s

Breed registries CFA, FIFe, GCCF, TICA

Weight range 3.5–7kg (8–15lb)

Grooming

Colours and patterns
Self, coloured, and tortie and tabby patterned points.

Known as the Himalayan in the USA, the Colourpoint Persian is the result of more than a decade of breeding programmes aimed at producing a longhair with Siamese markings. Round-faced and snub-nosed, with large eyes, a short, sturdy body, and long, lush fur, the Colourpoint has all the typical Persian characteristics. It is a cat that loves to be loved, although as a companion it is quiet and undemanding. Daily grooming is a must for this breed, as the dense, double coat is inclined to mat without regular attention.

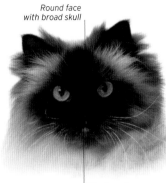

Round face with broad skull

Short, snub nose with pronounced stop between eyes

Face mask of contrasting seal colour

Seal point coat

Broad, stocky body

Large, round paws with long tufts between toes

Long, thick ivory-coloured coat over entire body

Large blue eyes

Small ears with rounded tips

Short, brush-like tail with seal pointing

Deep ruff

BALINESE

A VERY SPECIAL CAT THAT IS REFINED IN APPEARANCE BUT WITH HIDDEN STEEL

Place of origin USA

Date of origin 1950s

Breed registries CFA, FIFe, GCCF, TICA

Weight range 2.5–5kg (6–11lb)

Grooming

Colours and patterns
Seal, chocolate, blue, and lilac self colour points.

A longhaired version of the Siamese, the Balinese is an exquisite cat with the slender, graceful outlines of its relation draped in a flowing, silky coat. Records show that longhaired kittens have appeared occasionally among shorthaired Siamese litters for many decades, but it was not until the 1950s that some breeders began to develop the new look. The Balinese has an outgoing personality and is bursting with energy and curiosity. Although not as loud-voiced as the Siamese, it is attention-seeking, and also has a strong streak of mischief – owners of a Balinese would be well advised not to leave this cat to its own devices over long periods.

Clearly defined seal mask covers most of face

Long, straight nose with no break

Very large, wide-based ears

Almond-shaped deep blue eyes slant towards nose

Long, fine, close-lying lilac point coat

Seal point coat

Long, tapering, wedge-shaped head

Long, lithe, strong body

Plumed tail

Seal pointing on legs matches shading on body

Long, slender legs

BALINESE-JAVANESE

THIS CONFIDENT AND ATTENTION-SEEKING CAT DEMANDS A PLACE IN THE FAMILY

Place of origin	USA
Date of origin	1950s
Breed registries	CFA
Weight range	2.5–5kg (6–11lb)
Grooming	

Colours and patterns
Many point colours, in tabby and tortie patterns.

This enchanting cat is a development of the Balinese (opposite), the longhaired relation of the Siamese, with which it shares an identical breed standard in terms of conformation and coat quality. The difference between the two is the range of additional colours and patterns in the Javanese, which were acquired mostly through crosses with the Colourpoint Shorthair (p.58). Lithe and athletic despite its delicate appearance, the Javanese has a strong character to match. An affectionate, communicative cat, it loves to follow its owner around – when it is not prying into every nook and cranny of the house. The silky coat does not mat and is relatively easy to groom.

Clear, vivid blue eyes

Fine, silky, seal tortie-tabby point coat

Long, wedge-shaped head with flat skull

Long, thin, plumed tail

Small, neat, oval paws

Large, pointed ears

Long, graceful, muscular body

Shoulders and hips are same width

Slender, elegant neck

Ivory coat with seal tortie pointing

Long, slim-boned, legs with oval paws

YORK CHOCOLATE

THIS BREED IS SWEET AND LOVING, BUT A KEEN HUNTER OUTDOORS

Place of origin	USA
Date of origin	1980s
Breed registries	Other
Weight range	2.5–5kg (6–11lb)

Grooming

Colours and patterns
Self colour: chocolate, lavender; bicolour: chocolate and white, lavender and white.

The founding female of the York Chocolate breed came from New York State and was a dark chocolate brown, hence the breed's name. When kittens born to this cat had the same rich colouring, their owner developed an enthusiasm for continuing the line. Although still comparatively rare, the York Chocolate has attracted much attention at cat shows in North America. The breed includes bicolours with patches of chocolate or lavender. It is a gentle lap cat with an affectionate temperament and loves to be petted. In the home this soft-voiced breed will quietly make its presence felt by following its owner everywhere and joining in with anything that is going on.

Large, pointed ears

Almond-shaped eyes

Medium-long muzzle

Semi-long, silky chocolate and white coat with thin undercoat

Rounded head

Long, slender neck

Plumed tail tapers to a point

Long, well-built but not heavy body

Paws tufted between toes

ORIENTAL LONGHAIR

A TYPICAL ORIENTAL CAT THAT NEEDS PLENTY OF COMPANY AND AMUSEMENT

Place of origin	UK
Date of origin	1960s
Breed registries	CFA, FIFe, GCCF, TICA
Weight range	2.5–5kg (6–11lb)

Grooming

Colours and patterns
Many colours, including self, smoke, and shaded; tortie, tabby, and bicolour patterns.

Known originally as the British Angora, the Oriental Longhair was renamed in 2002 to avoid confusion with the Turkish Angora (p.178). The breed was developed in the 1960s in an attempt to re-create the silky-haired Angora cats that were favoured pets in Victorian households until ousted by the up-and-coming Persians. Breeding programmes included various longhaired Oriental cats, such as the Balinese (pp.156–7), producing what is in essence a longhaired Siamese – lithe-bodied and elegant but without colour points. Curious, playful, and highly active, the Oriental Longhair loves to be the centre of family attention, but often chooses one person with whom to form a close bond.

Striking, almond-shaped green eyes

Wide-based, triangular ears

Long, elegant neck

Fine, silky, semi-long coat with no undercoat

Rounded head

Chocolate coat colour

Long, angular, well-muscled body

Plumed, tapering tail

Slender legs with fine bone structure

Neat, oval paws

TIFFANIE

THIS EASY-GOING BREED MAKES AN IDEAL COMPANION FOR OWNERS OF ALL AGES

Place of origin UK

Date of origin 1980s

Breed registries GCCF

Weight range 3.5–6.5kg (8–14lb)

Grooming

Colours and patterns
All self and shaded colours; tabby and tortie patterns.

Formerly called the Asian Longhair, this cat is often confused with an American breed that has been known variously as the Tiffany, Chantilly, or Chantilly/Tiffany (opposite). It first appeared by chance as a longhaired variant of the Burmilla, a breed that itself originated as a happy accident following an unplanned mating between a European Burmese (p.39) and a Persian Chinchilla (p.140). The Tiffanie is a gentle, cuddly cat with a hint of mischief inherited from the Burmese side of its family. This cat is good at amusing itself with its own games, but is pleased if a human wants to join in. Sensitive and intelligent, the Tiffanie is said to be highly responsive to the moods of its owner.

Yellow-green eyes set well apart

Medium-long, silky coat darkens towards base of tail

Broad, wedge-shaped head

Fairly large, wide-based ears

Thick ruff around neck

Compact body with straight, muscular back

Blue-tipped silver coat

Long, plumed tail

Strong, medium-length legs

Oval paws

CHANTILLY/TIFFANY

A RARE BREED WITH A SOFT, FULL, RICHLY COLOURED COAT

Place of origin USA

Date of origin 1960s

Breed registries Other

Weight range 2.5–5kg (6–11lb)

Grooming

Colours and patterns
Black, blue, lilac, chocolate, cinnamon, and fawn; various tabby patterns.

The history of the Chantilly/Tiffany starts with a litter of chocolate-brown kittens born to two longhaired cats of unknown origin. A once widespread belief that the Burmese was included in the breed's ancestry has now been discounted. The various names registered for this cat during its development – Foreign Longhair, Tiffany, and Chantilly – caused much confusion, and the dual name is now the most commonly accepted. Although very attractive and possessing a sweet personality, the Chantilly/Tiffany has not yet achieved great popularity. It loves human companionship but asks for it politely, attracting attention with a soft trill.

High cheekbones

Longer ruff around neck

Silky, semi-long chocolate coat has minimal undercoat

Ears with rounded tips

Almond-shaped eyes slightly angled

Nose slopes to broad muzzle

Legs strong but not heavy

Medium-long body

Long tail is thickly plumed

BIRMAN

THIS CAT IS QUIET AND GENTLE BUT HIGHLY RESPONSIVE TO AN OWNER'S ATTENTION

Place of origin Myanmar (Burma)/France

Date of origin c.1920s

Breed registries CFA, FIFe, GCCF, TICA

Weight range 4.5-8kg (10-18lb)

Grooming

Colours and patterns
All colour points, with white feet.

With its distinctive colour points, this exquisite cat has the appearance of a longhaired Siamese, but the two breeds are unlikely to be closely related. According to a charming legend, Birmans descend from the sacred white cats once kept by priests in Myanmar (Burma), their colouring bestowed by mysterious supernatural powers. In reality, the breed was probably created in France in the 1920s, though the foundation cats may have been acquired from Myanmar. Long-bodied and sturdily built, the Birman has silky textured hair that does not mat like that of many longhaired cats.

Full cheeks and round muzzle

Well-developed jaw

Round blue eyes

Silky blue point coat

Roman nose

Strong, elongated body

Thick ruff around neck

Sturdy legs

Paws have white "gloves"

PEACEFUL PET
Gentle and sweet, the Birman is an exceptionally easy pet to live with. Even the long coat is not difficult to groom, as there is little undercoat to become tangled or clogged with loose hair.

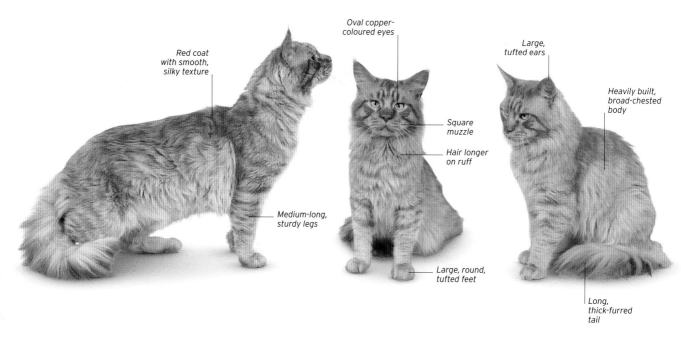

Oval copper-coloured eyes

Red coat with smooth, silky texture

Large, tufted ears

Heavily built, broad-chested body

Square muzzle

Hair longer on ruff

Medium-long, sturdy legs

Large, round, tufted feet

Long, thick-furred tail

MAINE COON

AN IMPRESSIVELY LARGE CAT THAT IS KIND-NATURED AND EASY TO KEEP

Place of origin	USA
Date of origin	1800s
Breed registries	CFA, FIFe, GCCF, TICA
Weight range	4–7.5kg (9–17lb)

Grooming

Colours and patterns
Many self colours and shades in tortie, tabby, and bicolour patterns.

Regarded as America's native cat, the Maine Coon is named after the New England state where it was first recognized. How the breed first arrived there has been explained in various entertaining but mostly improbable tales. Wilder versions of the Maine Coon's history put forward the theory that it descends from Scandinavian cats brought in by the Vikings, or claim that several cats of this type were sent to the USA by Marie Antoinette, anxious to preserve her pets during the French Revolution. The suggestion that the Maine Coon was originally a hybrid between feral cats and raccoons can definitely be discounted as a scientific impossibility, though the cat's bushy tail makes it easy to see how the idea might once have had credibility.

Huge and handsome, the Maine Coon has a thick, shaggy, waterproof coat that served it well in its earlier role as a farm cat, leading an outdoor life through harsh North American winters. Once highly regarded for its skills as a vermin-catcher, this breed has become a popular pet since the mid-20th century. Maine Coons have many endearing characteristics, including a tendency to act like kittens all their lives. Their voice, described by some as a bird-like chirrup, sounds surprisingly small for such a big cat. These cats are slow to mature and do not usually reach their full magnificent growth until about their fifth year.

SEASONAL COAT

A Maine Coon in full coat has an immense ruff, which is usually shaggier in males than in females. This provides excellent insulation and would have been a vital cold-weather accessory when Maine Coons were outdoor working cats. The coat changes seasonally, much of the thick undercoat being shed in summer.

WEATHERPROOF
The Maine Coon's massively thick coat keeps the cold out and warmth in. Even the long ear tufts are designed to protect the large, broad-based ears from the harshest weather.

RAGDOLL

THIS HUGE CAT IS REMARKABLY SWEET AND AMENABLE

Place of origin USA

Date of origin 1960s

Breed registries CFA, FIFe, GCCF, TICA

Weight range 4.5-9kg (10-20lb)

Grooming

Colours and patterns
Most self colours in tortie and tabby patterns; always pointed and bicolour or mitted.

The name is well chosen, as few cats are easier to handle or more ready to sit on a lap than a Ragdoll. One of the largest of all cat breeds, this cat has a confused history – supposedly, the original Ragdolls were developed from a litter of kittens, born in California, that became unusually limp and "floppy" when picked up. These cats love human company, will happily play with children, and are usually well disposed towards other pets. Ragdolls are not particularly athletic and, once past kittenhood, mostly prefer their games to be gentle. Moderate grooming is enough to keep their soft, silky fur free from tangles.

Large, oval, bright blue eyes

Very large, heavily boned body

Wide-set ears

Blue and white bicolour coat

Broad, wedge-shaped head

Seal bicolour coat becomes longer towards tail

Long, plumed tail

Long feathering on hindlegs

Long, silky guard hairs cover woolly undercoat

Fur shorter on lower legs

RAGAMUFFIN

A MASSIVELY BUILT, BIG-HEARTED, AND DELIGHTFULLY CALM CAT

Place of origin USA

Date of origin Late 20th century

Breed registries CFA, GCCF

Weight range 4.5–9kg (10–20lb)

Grooming

Colours and patterns
All self colours in bicolour, tortie, and tabby patterns.

This comparatively recent breed has a complicated history but it emerged as a new development of the better-known Ragdoll (opposite). The RagaMuffin is a huge cat, a true gentle giant that fits in placidly with families of all types. It thrives on affection and its docile temperament makes it an excellent pet for children. The RagaMuffin is not without a sense of fun and is easily persuaded to play with toys. This cat's dense, silky fur is not prone to matting, and short, regular grooming sessions will keep the coat in good order.

Dip in nose

Large eyes with characteristic sweet expression

Full cheeks

Long, plumed tail

Broad, rounded head

Wide-set ears with rounded tips

Heavily built, rectangular body

Thick, silky black and white coat does not mat easily

SOMALI

A CAT WITH DRAMATIC LOOKS, A GORGEOUS COAT, AND A COLOURFUL PERSONALITY

Place of origin USA

Date of origin 1960s

Breed registries CFA, FIFe, GCCF, TICA

Weight range 3.5–5.5kg (8–12lb)

Grooming

Colours and patterns
Various colours, some with silver tipping; tortie pattern; silver hairs always ticked.

This astoundingly beautiful breed is a longhaired relative of the Abyssinian (p.83). Neither the Somali nor its short-coated relation have any proven links with Africa to justify their names. The eye-catching coat of the Somali comes in a variety of rich colours and is exceptionally fine-haired. Most striking of all of the cat's features is its immense, bushy tail. Lively and insatiably curious, the Somali makes an amusing and engaging pet. Though highly affectionate and family friendly, this is not generally a lap cat; the Somali has too much energy to sit still for long.

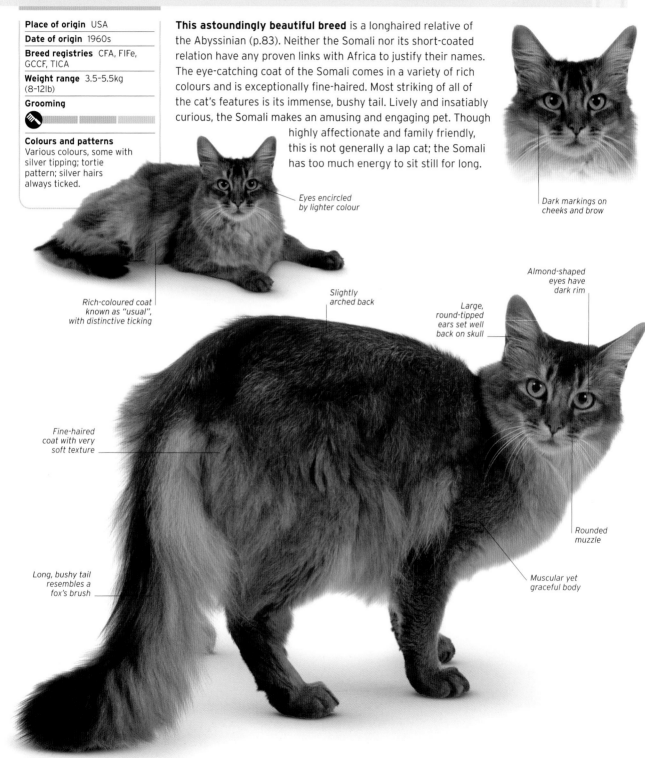

Dark markings on cheeks and brow

Eyes encircled by lighter colour

Rich-coloured coat known as "usual", with distinctive ticking

Slightly arched back

Almond-shaped eyes have dark rim

Large, round-tipped ears set well back on skull

Fine-haired coat with very soft texture

Rounded muzzle

Muscular yet graceful body

Long, bushy tail resembles a fox's brush

BRITISH LONGHAIR
THIS CHUNKY, HANDSOME CAT HAS A LONG, FLOWING COAT

Place of origin UK

Date of origin 1800s

Breed registries TICA

Weight range 4–8kg (9–18lb)

Grooming

Colours and patterns
Same colours and patterns as recognized in the British Shorthair.

This cat, known as the Lowlander in the USA and the Britanica in Europe, is the longer-haired cousin of the British Shorthair (pp.68–77). The two are identical in body shape, sharing the same sturdy build, massive head, and round face, and both come in the same range of colours. Not all pedigree cat registries regard the British Longhair as a separate breed. Regardless of its official status, this cat makes an excellent pet, as it has a calm, easy-going, people-loving temperament. The long coat needs moderate grooming to keep it tangle-free.

Short, broad nose

Large, round gold eyes set well apart

Prominent whisker pads

Full neck ruff

Short, thick, brush-like tail

Short, well-muscled back

Skull slightly flattened between widely spaced ears

Medium-long, dense cream coat

Long breeches on hindquarters

Lighter chest and underparts

Large, round paws

NEBELUNG

AN AFFECTIONATE BREED THAT LIKES A SECURE ROUTINE AND IS SHY WITH STRANGERS

Place of origin	USA
Date of origin	1980s
Breed registries	GCCF, TICA
Weight range	2.5-5kg (6-11lb)

Grooming

Colours and patterns
Blue, sometimes silver-tipped.

Developed in Denver, Colorado, in the late 20th century, the Nebelung is an outcross from the Russian Blue (pp.66-7), deliberately bred to re-create the longhaired blue cats that were popular in the Victorian era. The breed's name, taken from the German word *nebel* meaning haze or mist, is appropriate to its softly glistening coat. Naturally reserved and preferring a quiet environment, this cat may not settle well in a family of boisterous children. However, with sensitive handling, the Nebelung makes a devoted pet, anxious to keep its owners in sight and loving a lap to sit on.

Feathering behind ears

Slightly oval yellowish green eyes

Long, graceful body

Silver-tipped blue coat has soft sheen

Large ears continue wedge-shaped line of head

Prominent whisker pads

Heavily plumed tail

Ruff around neck

Shorter fur on lower legs

Hair tufts between toes

NORWEGIAN FOREST CAT

THIS CAT IS BIG, TOUGH, AND BURLY BUT ALSO GENTLE AND WELL-MANNERED

Place of origin Norway

Date of origin 1950s

Breed registries CFA, FIFe, GCCF, TICA

Weight range 3–9kg (7–20lb)

Grooming

Colours and patterns
Most self colours, shades, and patterns.

Cats have been known in Scandinavia since Viking times, being kept as useful pest destroyers in homesteads and villages. The Norwegian Forest Cat cannot claim direct descent from these ancestors, as the breed was developed fully only in the 1970s, but its characteristics are recognizably those of the cats familiar for centuries on Norwegian farms. This magnificent cat's long double coat, a natural insulation against bitter northern winters, may become much thicker in colder months as the undercoat reaches full density. Surprisingly, this does not mean extra winter grooming for owners, although shedding is likely to be heavy in spring.

Broad-based ears rounded at tip

Almond-shaped green eyes

Triangular head

Silver tabby coat

Long, plumed tail

Nose straight in profile

Well-muscled, powerful body

Short, strong neck

Thick silver tortie-tabby coat

White markings on chest, face, and legs

Thick tufts between toes

TURKISH VAN

A PLAYFUL BREED WITH AN UNUSUAL LIKING FOR WATER GAMES

Place of origin Turkey/UK (modern breed)

Date of origin Pre-1700

Breed registries CFA, FIFe, GCCF, TICA,

Weight range 3-8.5kg (7-19lb)

Grooming

Colours and patterns
White with darker colours on head and tail.

The predecessors of this cat, named after the Lake Van area of eastern Turkey, may have existed for hundreds of years around the region now known as the Middle East. The modern Turkish Van was first developed in the UK in the 1950s, and breeding cats have since been exported to other countries, though they remain uncommon. A Turkish Van is not the ideal choice for an owner who wants a peaceful lap cat – zestful and fun-loving, this cat enjoys a game, especially if the family joins in. Many Turkish Vans also love dabbling about with water, and some are reputed to be confident swimmers.

Pink nose leather

Ears set well apart

Soft, water-resistant white coat has no undercoat

Large amber eyes with pink rims

Auburn Van markings restricted to head and tail

Prominent cheekbones

Feathered tail

Deep chest

Broad, well-muscled body, especially in males

Long legs with fairly large, rounded paws

TURKISH VANKEDISI

THIS RARE BREED IS AN ALL-WHITE VARIANT OF THE TURKISH VAN CAT

Place of origin	Eastern Turkey
Date of origin	Pre-1700
Breed registries	GCCF
Weight range	3–8.5kg (7–19lb)
Grooming	

Colours and patterns
Pure white only.

This cat has its origins in the same region of Turkey as the Turkish Van (opposite), and it is distinguished from that breed only by the lack of the typical Van markings on its snow-white coat. In all other respects, it shares the characteristics of its relation. The Turkish Vankedisi is rare anywhere in the world and is much prized in its native country. Like many all-white cats, the breed has a tendency to inherit deafness but it is nonetheless strong and active. Its pleasant temperament makes this cat an affectionate companion but it demands plenty of attention.

Long, straight nose

Silky, snow-white coat

Long hair inside ears

Fairly broad, wedge-shaped head

Odd-coloured eyes

Pink rim around eyes

Long, muscular legs

Round, tufted paws

Long, bushy tail

TURKISH ANGORA

THIS BREED IS DELICATE TO LOOK AT BUT HAS A STRONG CHARACTER

Place of origin	Turkey
Date of origin	16th century
Breed registries	CFA, FIFe, TICA
Weight range	2.5–5kg (6–11lb)

Grooming

Colours and patterns
Many self colours and shades; patterns include tabby, tortie, and bicolour.

Records indicate that this native Turkish breed probably reached France and the UK some time around the 17th century. Widely used in the development of other longhaired cats such as Persians, especially during the early 20th century, the Turkish Angora as a breed became so diluted that it almost ceased to exist except in its own country. In Turkey, the cat had been given greater protection, and by the 1950s purebred Angoras were being sent around Europe and to the USA. Still rare, the Angora is one of the most exquisite of all longhaired cats, with its fine bone structure and exceptionally soft, glistening coat.

Small- to medium-sized head

Blue-cream tortie coat

Fine-boned, slender yet muscular body

Slender, graceful neck

Small, rounded paws usually tufted between the toes

Large, tufted ears set high on head

Almond-shaped, slightly slanting green eyes

Fine, silky, shimmering black coat, with no undercoat

Long, tapering, brush-like tail

Long legs

SIBERIAN

A LARGE, HEAVY-COATED CAT THAT IS SLOW TO REACH FULL MATURITY

Place of origin Russia

Date of origin 1980s

Breed registries CFA, FIFe, GCCF, TICA

Weight range 4.5–9kg (10–20lb)

Grooming

Colours and patterns
All colours and patterns.

This forest cat is native to Russia, where it has probably been around for centuries in varying forms. Breeding Siberians to standard did not begin until the 1980s, and full breed recognition did not come until a decade later after a number of cats had been imported to the USA. Although still rare, the Siberian cat is gaining popularity for its handsome looks and engaging personality. It may take five years or more for a Siberian to attain full growth. Despite its moderately hefty build in adulthood, this breed is highly athletic and loves to leap and play.

Round-tipped ears tilt slightly forward

Short, well-rounded muzzle

Unique triple coat

Thick ruff around neck

Eyes almost round, slightly angled towards base of ear, and may be odd-coloured

Silver-spotted tabby coat

Tail shorter than body length

White markings on chest, face, and legs

Limbs heavily boned

Large, round, tufted white paws

NEVA MASQUERADE

A MAGNIFICENT COLOURPOINTED CAT WITH AN ULTRA-THICK COAT

Place of origin Russia
Date of origin 1970s
Breed registries FIFe
Weight range 4.5–9kg (10–20lb)
Grooming

Colours and patterns
Various colourpoints, including seal, blue, red, cream, tabby, and tortie.

This breed is the colourpoint version of the Siberian (p.179), a forest cat that has a long history in Russia. The Neva Masquerade is named after the Neva River in St Petersburg, where it was first developed. Combining strength with gentleness, this substantially built cat makes an excellent family pet and has a reputation for becoming particularly attached to children. The immensely thick coat of the Neva Masquerade, which has a double-layered undercoat, is not inclined to form mats or knots, so grooming is not a difficult task, although it does need to be done regularly.

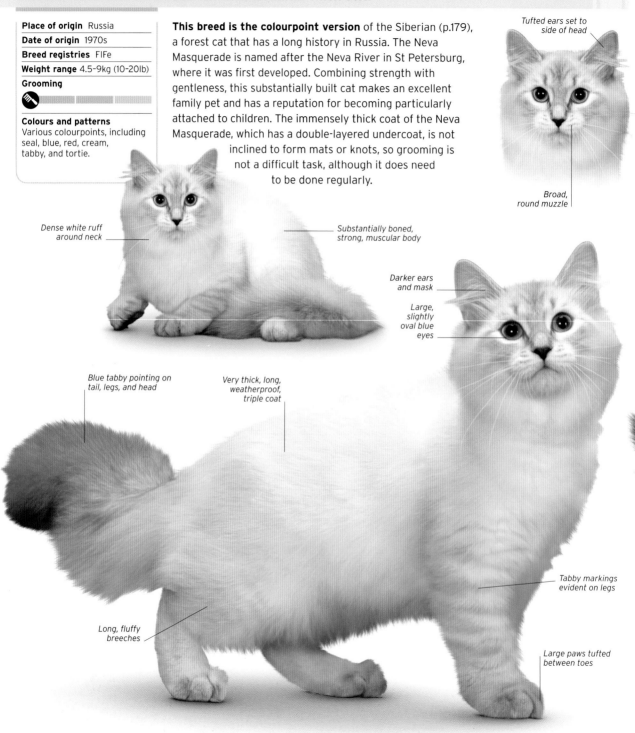

Tufted ears set to side of head

Broad, round muzzle

Dense white ruff around neck

Substantially boned, strong, muscular body

Darker ears and mask

Large, slightly oval blue eyes

Blue tabby pointing on tail, legs, and head

Very thick, long, weatherproof, triple coat

Tabby markings evident on legs

Long, fluffy breeches

Large paws tufted between toes

MUNCHKIN

A DEVOTED CAT WITH VERY SHORT LEGS BUT A FULL ZEST FOR LIVING

Place of origin USA

Date of origin 1980s

Breed registries TICA

Weight range 2.5–4kg (6–9lb)

Grooming

Colours and patterns
All colours, shades, and patterns.

The extraordinarily short legs of the Munchkin are the result of a chance mutation. This breed appears to have escaped the spinal problems sometimes associated with very short legs in dogs such as the Dachshund, and having a low-to-the-ground stature does not inhibit its general mobility. In fact, Munchkins can run extremely fast, and are energetic and playful. These confident and inquisitive cats make sociable family pets. As well as the silky, semi-longhaired version, there is also a shorthaired Munchkin (p.101), and both come in an almost endless variety of colours and patterns. The Munchkin longhair needs regular grooming to prevent the coat from matting.

Flat forehead

Walnut-shaped golden eyes set wide apart, have an alert expression

Muscular body

Whisker pads often prominent

Exceptionally short legs

Ears with slightly rounded tips

Well-defined cheekbones

Silky, weather-resistant coat

Back with slight slope from shoulders to rump

Tail is same length as body, with rounded tip

Shaggy breeches

NAPOLEON

THIS SHORT, ROUND CAT COMES WITH A LUXURY FUR COAT

Place of origin	USA
Date of origin	1990s
Breed registries	TICA
Weight range	3–7.5kg (7–17lb)

Grooming

Colours and patterns
All colours, shades, and patterns, including colourpoint.

A sturdy, low-to-the-ground cat, the Napoleon longhair is a hybrid specially bred to combine the very short legs of the Munchkin (p.181) with the luxuriant fur of the Persian (pp.136–55), including versions with a colourpointed coat. There is also a shorthaired variant of the Napoleon. This breed is very active, despite its short stature, and has plenty of character. The Persian influence has ensured that the Napoleon likes spending time as a lap cat too, and it loves to be made a fuss of, although it is not over-demanding.

Round head with full cheeks

Round, wide-open eyes

Smallish ears with rounded tips

Muzzle fairly short with round whisker pads

Semi-long white coat stands out from body

Ruff around neck

Short nose with well-defined stop

Long, plumed tail

Shaggy breeches

Short, firm legs

SCOTTISH FOLD

A CHARMING, SOCIABLE CAT WITH A DELIGHTFUL "OWL-FACED" APPEARANCE

Place of origin UK/USA

Date of origin 1960s

Breed registries CFA, TICA

Weight range 2.5-6kg (6-13lb)

Grooming

Colours and patterns
Most self colours and shades; most tabby, tortie, and colourpoint patterns.

The tightly folded-down ears of this rare breed and its shorthaired relation (pp.106-7) are due to a genetic mutation seen in no other cat. Descended from a folded-ear Scottish farm cat, the Fold is not recognized as a breed by the leading cat registry in the UK because of concerns about genetically linked health problems, although it has been more successful in the USA. The diverse coat colours of the Scottish Fold come from the many different outcrosses, including domestic non-pedigree cats, that were selected to develop the breed. The dense coat is of variable length and is enhanced by a thick ruff and a huge, plumed tail.

Rounded golden eyes

Prominent whisker pads

Long, plumed tail

Medium-sized, well-padded body

Small ears fold tightly forward to fit over skull like a cap

Thick ruff, especially with winter coat

Tufted toes

Rounded head with firm jaw

Long, full blue-cream and white coat

Short, broad, slightly curved nose

White markings on legs extend to chest and face

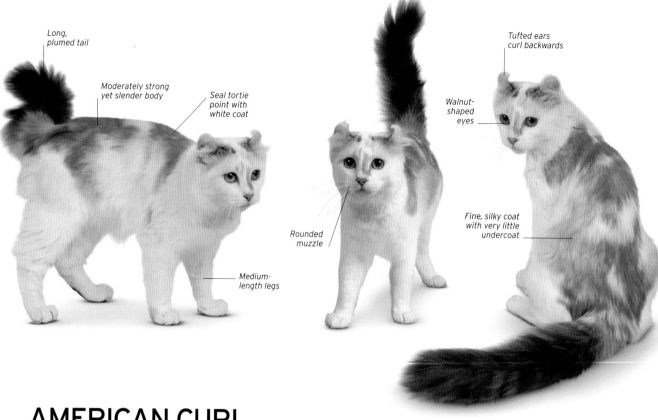

Long, plumed tail

Moderately strong yet slender body

Seal tortie point with white coat

Medium-length legs

Rounded muzzle

Tufted ears curl backwards

Walnut-shaped eyes

Fine, silky coat with very little undercoat

AMERICAN CURL

A RARE BREED WITH HIGHLY DISTINCTIVE CURLED-BACK EARS

Place of origin USA	
Date of origin 1980s	
Breed registries CFA, FIFe, TICA	
Weight range 3–5kg (7–11lb)	
Grooming	

Colours and patterns
All self colours and shades; patterns include colourpoint, tabby, and tortie.

This breed has its origins in a stray cat with a long, black coat and oddly curled ears that was adopted off the street by a family in California in 1981. The cat, a female, went on to produce a litter of curly eared kittens, and the rare mutation aroused widespread interest among both breeders and geneticists. Programmes for the planned development of the American Curl, in both longhaired and shorthaired (p.109) variants, began remarkably quickly, and the future of the new breed was secured.

In an American Curl, the ears curve backwards to a greater or lesser extent, the arc of the curl ideally somewhere between 90 and 180 degrees. The cartilage is firm, not floppy, and the ears of these cats should never be manipulated. At birth, all Curl kittens have straight ears, but in about 50 per cent of them the characteristic curve begins to take shape within a few days, reaching its full arc by the time the cat is about three or four months old. Cats whose ears remain straight are of value in breeding programmes, as their use helps to keep the American Curl genetically healthy.

The longhaired Curl has a silky coat that lies close to the body. There is very little undercoat, which makes grooming easy and means minimal shedding. A further embellishment in the longhair is the lovely, long, plumed tail.

Alert, intelligent, and affectionate, the American Curl has an attractive personality and is an excellent family pet. This cat is gentle and soft-voiced, but not at all shy about pestering its owner for attention.

HIGHLANDER
THIS RARE BREED WITH STRIKING LOOKS IS FAMILY-LOVING AND PLAYFUL

Place of origin	North America
Date of origin	2000s
Breed registries	TICA
Weight range	4.5-11kg (10-25lb)
Grooming	

Colours and patterns
All colours in any tabby pattern, including colourpoints.

With its thick, almost shaggy coat, the Highlander longhair looks like a small lynx, although there are no wild cats in its breeding. This curly eared newcomer on the cat scene is large and powerfully built, but moves with grace. Full of life and energy, the Highlander longhair is not content to stay in the background, and owners – and other pets – will be pestered constantly to play. Nonetheless, this is a gentle, affectionate cat that gets on well with children. The heavy coat needs regular grooming to prevent mats and tangling. There is a shorthaired version (p.109) of the Highlander that is easier to maintain.

Sloping forehead

Prominent whisker pads

Long, soft, chocolate-spotted tabby coat

Substantial, well-boned legs

Curled ears

Naturally short tail is curled

Nose and muzzle look blunt in profile

Long, strong, flexible hindlegs

Longer, lighter hair on belly

Medium to large paws thickly tufted between toes

JAPANESE BOBTAIL

THIS CAT IS ALWAYS ON THE GO, "TALKATIVE", AND INQUISITIVE

Place of origin Japan

Date of origin c.17th century

Breed registries CFA, TICA

Weight range 2.5–4kg (6–9lb)

Grooming

Colours and patterns
All self colours in bicolour, tabby, and tortie patterns.

Both longhaired and shorthaired (p.110) Japanese Bobtails appear to have been favoured pets in Japan for several hundred years. In the 1960s the first of these charismatic and unusual cats were imported to the USA, where the modern breed was developed. Japanese Bobtails are loving and lovable, but with their outgoing and energetic natures they are not for the owner who wants a lap cat. There are many variations on the short, plumed tail, which can curve or bend in any direction. The longhaired coat falls softly over the body and is relatively easy to groom.

Large, oval eyes set at a slant

Long nose with slight stop

Unique kinked "rabbit" tail

Long coat parts along top line

Brown mackerel-tabby colour patches

Elegantly sculpted head with high cheekbones

Ears set wide apart

Longer coat on hindquarters

Hindlegs longer than forelegs

Soft, silky white coat with minimal undercoat

Long, slender legs with oval paws

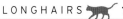

KURILIAN BOBTAIL

A RARE SHORT-TAILED BREED THAT THRIVES ON COMPANY AND AFFECTION

Place of origin Kuril Islands, North Pacific

Date of origin 20th century (modern breed)

Breed registries FIFe, TICA

Weight range 3–4.5kg (7–10lb)

Grooming

Colours and patterns
Most self colours, shades, and patterns, including tabby.

This solidly handsome cat takes its name from the Kuril Islands, an archipelago in the North Pacific, where it is thought to have its origins. As both Russia and Japan have laid claim to various of these islands, it is uncertain from which country the Kurilian Bobtail longhair really comes. The breed has been popular on the Russian mainland since the 1950s, as has the shorthaired version (p.111), but it is uncommon elsewhere and particularly rare in the USA. The Kurilian Bobtail adores family life and can never get enough fuss and attention from its owner, although it has a strong streak of independence.

Bright, oval gold eyes

Prominent whisker pads

Body large but compact and well proportioned

Short tail is kinked

Medium-sized ears wide at base

Large, rounded head

Cobby body shape

Silky, semi-long red-silver mackerel tabby coat

Banding on legs

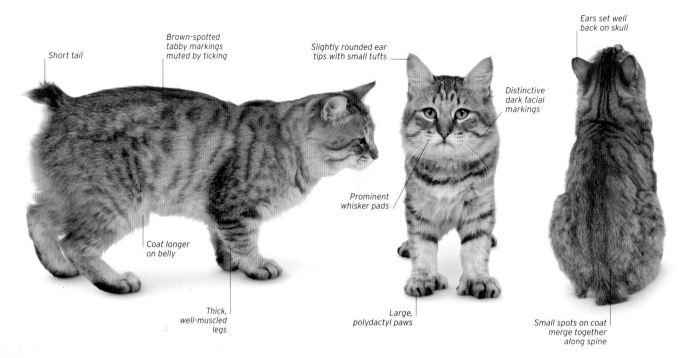

Short tail

Brown-spotted tabby markings muted by ticking

Slightly rounded ear tips with small tufts

Ears set well back on skull

Distinctive dark facial markings

Prominent whisker pads

Coat longer on belly

Thick, well-muscled legs

Large, polydactyl paws

Small spots on coat merge together along spine

PIXIEBOB

THIS LARGE BREED RESEMBLES THE WILD BOBCAT OF NORTH AMERICA

Place of origin	USA
Date of origin	1980s
Breed registries	TICA
Weight range	4–8kg (9–18lb)
Grooming	

Colours and patterns
Brown spotted tabby only.

This relatively new breed has a similar appearance to the bobcat, native to the mountains of North America's Pacific coast. The resemblance is deliberate – the Pixiebob's characteristics having been developed by breeders catering for a growing fashion in domestic cats that look like their wild cousins. Lynx-like features include a thick, double tabby-spotted coat that stands out from the body; tufted ears; a heavy brow; and facial hair that grows in "sideburns". The tail varies in length and may be long and brush-like, although only short-tailed cats are eligible for showing. A shorthaired variation of the Pixiebob (p.116) creates much the same wildcat illusion.

The founding father of this breed was an exceptionally tall, bobtailed tabby that bred with an ordinary domestic female cat, sired bobtailed kittens with a special look – one of them, christened "Pixie", passed her name to the breed.

Powerfully built, with a swaggering air, Pixiebobs are active and athletic. However, they are also relaxed and sociable cats that take happily to family life, enjoy playing with older children, and are usually tolerant of other pets. Pixiebobs like being with people and many enjoy outdoor walks on a lead.

FAMILY CHARACTERISTICS

The kitten seen below has its mother's short hair but the bobtail and polydactyly (extra toes) of its longhaired father (main photos). This is the only breed in which polydactyly is allowed in show cats.

CYMRIC

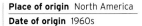

AN EXCELLENT FAMILY COMPANION, THIS BREED IS CALM BUT EASILY PERSUADED TO PLAY

Place of origin	North America
Date of origin	1960s
Breed registries	FIFe, TICA
Weight range	3.5–5.5kg (8–12lb)
Grooming	

Colours and patterns
All colours, shades, and patterns.

Developed in Canada, the Cymric is a long-coated variant of the tailless Manx (p.115). Sturdy and round-bodied, the breed, which is sometimes referred to as the Longhaired Manx, differs from its relative only in the length of its silky coat. Muscular hindquarters and long hindlegs give the Cymric a powerful jump – it can spring up onto high places with ease. Cymrics have an affectionate nature, frequently forming close attachments to their human family. They make intelligent and entertaining companions and appreciate plenty of attention from their owners.

Prominent whisker pads

Ruff around neck extends to shoulders

Thick breeches on hindlegs

Coat shorter on lower legs

Short back slopes gently down towards rump

White, glossy double coat lies smoothly on body

Large, round eyes slightly angled

Well-rounded rump lacks tail

Well-muscled hindquarters and legs

Sturdy forelegs shorter than hindlegs

AMERICAN BOBTAIL
A WILD CAT LOOKALIKE WITH A HOME-LOVING PERSONALITY

Place of origin USA

Date of origin 1960s

Breed registries CFA, TICA

Weight range 3–7kg (7–15lb)

Grooming

Colours and patterns
All colours, shades, and patterns.

According to a widely accepted opinion, the origins of this true native American cat can be traced to the naturally short-tailed, feral cats found free-roaming in various US states. The breed also has a short-coated cousin (p.113). The large, powerfully built Bobtail longhair has the alert air of a wild cat, but it is entirely benign and a good family pet. It is renowned for being tolerant of children and staying calm and friendly even with strangers. The Bobtail's long coat does not mat, so moderate grooming is all that is required.

Distinct brow above eyes

Alert "wild cat" expression

Chocolate spotted tabby coat

Short, slightly curved tail

Large, deep-set, almost almond-shaped eyes

Non-matting, easy-to-groom, classic brown tabby coat

Well-built, muscular body

Hips as wide as chest

Prominent whisker pads

Legs substantially boned

SELKIRK REX

THIS BREED HAS WILD CURLS AND AN ENDEARINGLY HUGGABLE PERSONALITY

Place of origin USA

Date of origin 1980s

Breed registries CFA, TICA

Weight range 3.5–5kg (8–11lb)

Grooming

Colours and patterns
All colours, shades, and patterns.

The breed originated with an odd curly-coated female kitten, discovered among an otherwise normal litter in an animal rescue centre in Montana, USA. Adopted as something of a curiosity, this cat went on to produce curly offspring and lay the foundations for the Selkirk Rex. Through planned matings with both Persians and short-coated breeds, longhaired and shorthaired (pp.124–5) lines were developed. These sweet-tempered, placid cats are almost irresistibly cuddly, and fortunately they are very happy to accept attention. Regular grooming of the Selkirk Rex longhair is essential, but owners should avoid over-vigorous brushing, as this can straighten out the curls.

Nose has well-defined stop

Round-cheeked, broad head

Short, square muzzle with full whisker pads

Longer white ruff around neck

Thick tail with rounded tip

Large, round blue eyes

Straight back rises slightly towards rear

Brittle curly whiskers

Medium-large, heavily boned body

Soft, loose, seal and white curls cover entire body

Large, round white paws

URAL REX

A LITTLE-KNOWN BREED, THIS CAT IS SAID TO BE QUIET AND GOOD WITH FAMILIES

Place of origin	Russia
Date of origin	1940s
Breed registries	Other
Weight range	3.5–7kg (8–15lb)

Grooming

Colours and patterns
Various colours and patterns, including tabby.

Although this cat was not generally recognized until fairly late in the 20th century, it is possibly one of the oldest of the rex breeds and is thought to have been in existence in the Ural region of Russia since the late 1940s. The Ural Rex longhair has a medium-long coat that falls in waves over its entire body. This rare cat comes in a shorter-haired version (p.122), which is also far from common. As test breeding has shown, the genetic mutation responsible for the Ural Rex's wavy coat appears to be very different from that found in other, better-known, rex cats, such as the Cornish Rex (p.127) and Devon Rex (pp.128–9).

Ears have rounded tips

Large, slanted, oval eyes

Pronounced cheekbones

Slender, relatively short muscular body

Slim legs

Tail tapers to rounded tip

Oval white paws

Short, broad, wedge-shaped head

Semi long chocolate coat lies in loose, elastic waves

LAPERM

THIS CLEVER AND CAPTIVATING CAT ADORES HUMAN COMPANY

Place of origin	USA
Date of origin	1980s
Breed registries	CFA, TICA
Weight range	3.5–5kg (8–11lb)
Grooming	

Colours and patterns
All colours, shades, and patterns.

An ordinary farm cat in Oregon, USA, produced the curly coated kittens that led to the development of the LaPerm. The unique coat of this shaggy but graceful cat varies considerably from soft waves to bouncy, corkscrew curls. There is also a shorthaired version (p.123). Long-legged and agile, LaPerms are active cats, but will readily accommodate their owners by switching from playing games to purring on a lap.

The LaPerm is not difficult to groom, as it has very little undercoat to shed or mat. Regular combing is the best way to keep the curls in good order.

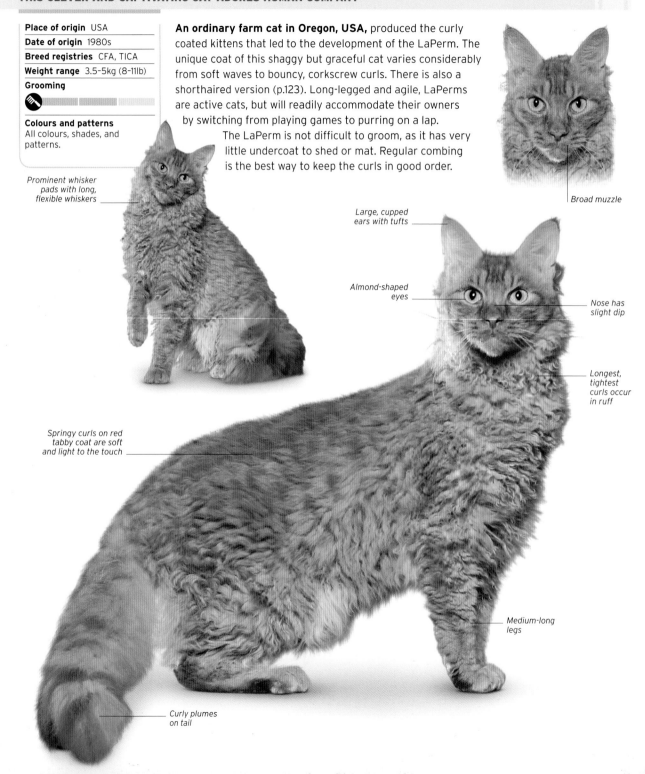

Prominent whisker pads with long, flexible whiskers

Broad muzzle

Large, cupped ears with tufts

Almond-shaped eyes

Nose has slight dip

Longest, tightest curls occur in ruff

Springy curls on red tabby coat are soft and light to the touch

Medium-long legs

Curly plumes on tail

HOUSECAT - LONGHAIR

REGARDLESS OF THEIR ANCESTRY, THESE CATS HAVE UNDENIABLE GLAMOUR

Non-pedigree cats with long hair are less common than their shorthaired counterparts. In some of them, the clues to their origins are obvious. A dense, woolly undercoat, stocky body, and a round, flattened face are likely to be inherited from a Persian. The ancestry of others remains a mystery in a confusion of variable coat lengths, mixed colours, and indeterminate patterns. Longhaired housecats rarely have the extravagantly thick coats seen in the show ring, but many of them are very beautiful.

BROWN TABBY
Long fur tends to blur tabby patterning. This cat has a semilong coat marked with the pattern known as "classic" tabby, which on a shorter coat would appear as boldly defined, dark whorls.

Faint tabby markings

Greenish-gold eyes

Brownish tinge to ruff

CREAM AND WHITE
Cream – a diluted form of red – is an unusual colour in the average housecat. This one has "ghost" tabby markings, which cat fanciers try to eliminate in pedigrees by breeding only the very palest creams.

BLACK
Jet-black was among the first colours to be popular in longhairs. In random-bred cats there are likely to be slight tinges of brown or tabby pattern in the coat.

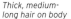

Thick, medium-long hair on body

RED AND WHITE TABBY
Most owners of a red tabby are likely to refer to their pet as a "ginger" cat. This colour is much sought after and can often be just as deep and rich in non-pedigree cats as it is in pure-breds.

Round face suggests Persian influence

SILVER AND WHITE
Rarely seen in the domestic housecat, silver is the effect of a white coat tipped with darker colour at the end of each hair. Depending on their degree of tipping, pedigree silver cats are sometimes known as chinchillas.

CARE AND BEHAVIOUR

PREPARING FOR ARRIVAL

Is your house ready for a cat or kitten? Before bringing a new pet home, take a good look around and ask yourself a few key questions: is there anywhere you don't want your cat to go; is there anything that could be hazardous to a cat; and which of your own habits might you or your family need to change when you have a cat? A little preparation will turn your home into a safe environment for the new arrival.

A kitten is life changing

Become cat-aware

Cats are inquisitive and athletic, and you should take this into account when evaluating your home. If you regularly leave doors and windows open, assess whether your cat could escape through them or enter areas you want to keep cat-free – and close them when necessary. Also, start looking behind you when going through a door, since a cat can easily slip through a gap at your feet. Close the doors of washing machines and tumble dryers when not in use, and always check the whereabouts of your cat before switching on.

Safety indoors

Cats love climbing, so remove breakable or valuable objects from low tables or shelves that they could leap on to. Be aware of possible pathways that would allow your cat to reach high shelves or work surfaces, and move furniture accordingly. Stools, standard lamps, wall hangings, and curtains are all scalable to a cat. Consider temporarily putting double-sided sticky tape, plastic sheeting, or aluminium foil around the edges of furniture you want to remain off limits until your cat learns to leave them alone; cats dislike the textures and will avoid stepping on them. Climbing and scratching are entirely natural behaviours for a cat, so make sure you provide outlets for these activities, such as a scratching pole and something safe for him to climb on to.

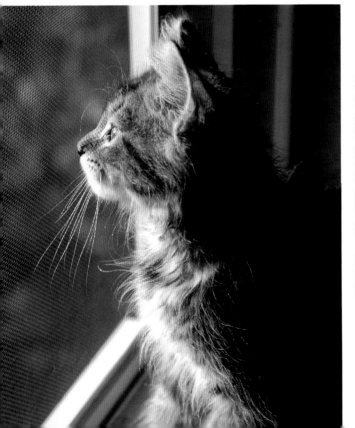

TOP TIP

Household chemicals are an obvious hazard. Keep them securely shut away in places a cat cannot reach. Mop up spills straight away. Also check whether any products are toxic to cats – for example carpet cleaners and bug control sprays. Do the same in any garage or shed that a cat could access. Even seemingly innocuous substances may be dangerous to cats, especially as their first instinct is to lick themselves clean if they get something on their coat or paws.

WINDOW SCREENS

Fitting window screens will enable you to leave windows open for fresh air and in hot weather, safe in the knowledge that your cat cannot escape.

OUTDOOR THREATS

FOXES   SNAKES   OTHER CATS   FIREWORKS   SUNBURN (WHITE CATS)

TOP TIPS

■ **Keep your cat indoors** during firework displays. Close doors and windows, mask the noise with music, and let your cat hide if he wants to. Don't reassure him, as this may be taken as a sign that you too are afraid. A pheromone plug-in may help your cat to stay calm.

■ **Cat sunblock** can be bought from pet shops. Cats with white coats or patches of white are susceptible to sunburn, as the skin under the fur is also pale. Use only cat-friendly sunblock.

NATURALLY CURIOUS
Cats will inspect and explore whatever and wherever they can. Make sure cupboards cannot be entered, and always put away sharp knives, scissors, pins, and tacks.

Beware of leaving small objects lying around: cats can swallow or choke on things such as toys, bottle caps, pen tops, and erasers. Tuck away wiring on electrical appliances and pull up dangling flexes so that your cat cannot drag a lamp or iron on to himself. Fit unused electrical sockets with childproof covers.

Safety outdoors

After assessing your home, carry out a "safety audit" of your garden or yard. Remove sharp, potentially harmful objects and prevent access to sheds and greenhouses. Even if you try to secure your garden from animal intruders, you will always have some "visitors". Foxes are usually wary of mature cats

and their claws, but they may harm kittens. Snakes are an issue in some places, mainly because cats prey on them and sometimes get bitten in the process. There are cat-friendly snake-repellent products on the market. Always examine your pet carefully after a fight with a neighbourhood cat, in case he has injuries that need a vet's attention. In urban areas, the greatest threat will be from traffic, so do your best to prevent your cat from being able to reach the road.

Dangerous plants

Some plants are toxic to cats if eaten (see below). Remove these dangerous plants from the garden. Keep houseplants off the floor and low tables, and cover the soil with chippings or pebbles to discourage digging. If your cat must nibble indoors, buy special cat grass plants from nurseries and keep them away from other plants to avoid confusion.

DANGEROUS PLANTS

INDOORS
- Dieffenbachia
- Poinsettia
- Mistletoe
- Lily
- Cactus
- Potted bulbs – crocus, daffodils
- Philodendron

OUTDOORS
- Azalea
- Hydrangea
- Nightshade
- Oleander
- Nicotiana
- Tomato leaves
- Potato leaves
- Rhododendron
- Yew
- Monkshood

Equipment for your cat

If you are a new cat owner, you'll need to buy a certain amount of equipment for your pet's comfort and well-being. These items include a bed, a litter tray, feeding and drinking bowls, and a scratching post. It's tempting to go for the latest "must have" items, but think carefully about whether your cat really needs such things. Start with good-quality basic items that are within your budget, since the initial outlay on your cat will quickly mount up. You can think about treating him to more sophisticated products later on.

Bed and bedding

Felines will take a catnap anywhere that takes their fancy, but like most animals they really appreciate somewhere that is exclusively their territory. Choose a round or oval, washable, soft-sided bed that is not too big. A blanket or old cushion can be added if your cat is not yet fully grown.

HANGING AROUND
Suspended from a radiator, this cat bed provides your pet with a warm, cosy place to sleep.

Basket style

Tent style

CAT BEDS
Beds come in a wide range of styles. If you know what kind of bed your cat used before joining your family, choose that type; otherwise, try to match the bed style with what you know of his character.

Litter trays

Open, covered, manual, automatic, self-cleaning – the choice of litter trays is ultimately down to you. However, if you are acquiring an older cat, stick to the type of tray with which he is familiar: a cat used to an open tray, for example, is likely to be reluctant to change to a covered one. Choosing the right litter material may involve some trial and error before you find a brand that your cat likes using and that meets your own requirements for cleaning. You can also add deodorizers to the litter. These come as sprays, powders, or granules; avoid scented products, as these may deter your cat from using the tray. The best deodorizers use enzymes to break down smells. A plastic scoop will be useful for removing clumps of urine and stools from the litter. Always wash the scoop after using it.

Litter tray

Scoop

Clay

Fibre pellets

WHICH LITTER TO CHOOSE?

■ **Ask the breeder** which litter the kitten is used to and stick with the same type.

■ **Clay** is the most popular type of litter, because it absorbs moisture quickly and clumps are easy to remove.

■ **Fibre pellets** are very absorbent products and are biodegradable.

■ **Non-absorbent** litter needs to be used in conjunction with a special tray that drains the urine into a collecting unit. Faeces need to be removed and disposed of, but the litter material itself can be washed and reused.

■ **Earth and sand** are popular choices for most cats. However, they may not be suitable for use in flats or houses without gardens, because they are bulky to store and are not biodegradable.

Food and water bowls

Bowls should be sturdy and stable enough not to tip over if trodden on. They should not be too deep and need to be wider than the cat's whiskers. Wash bowls at least once a day. Remove "wet" food after the cat has finished eating. If you feed

Plastic

Steel

FOOD BOWLS
There are many cat bowls to choose from. Make sure you pick one that is easy to clean. A rubber base can help stop the bowl sliding when your cat is eating.

your cat tinned food, buy an extra can opener that you can reserve solely for opening cat food. Use plastic lids to cover any partly used cans stored in the fridge. There are also automatic feeding stations available that operate on a timer. They flip open a lid at your cat's mealtime – a useful asset if you are going out and don't want to break the cat's routine.

Scratching posts

Providing a place for your cat to scratch is essential if you don't want your furniture or carpets ruined. Cats need to scratch every day to help wear away the outer sheaths of their claws. Scratching is also a way of marking territory. Scratching posts usually comprise a flat, rough-carpeted base and an upright post covered in coiled rope, often topped by a carpeted platform (p.235). Make sure the post is tall enough for your cat to get a really good stretch – preferably at least 30cm (1ft) high. Locate the post close to where your cat usually sleeps, since cats do most of their stretching and scratching immediately after waking up.

Collars and ID

It is important to get your cat tagged with a microchip. These tiny devices are no bigger than a grain of rice and are inserted by a vet under the loose skin at the back of the neck. Each chip has a unique number that can be detected when it is scanned by a reader. When the number is fed into a database, your contact details will come up. It's worth doing this even if you have an indoor cat - cats are superb at escaping and may take advantage of an open window or a loose door on a cat carrier. All outdoor cats should have

a collar with an ID tag giving your name and address, along with a telephone number or email address. The collar must be loose enough for you slip two fingers underneath. Many collars have an elasticated section or quick-release snap that allows the cat to escape if the collar becomes snagged.

Cat carriers

A cat carrier is the safest way to transport your cat. Whether it is made of plastic, wire, or traditional basketwork, it must be large enough for your cat to turn around in. A blanket or cushion can be put inside to keep him warm and comfy. To get your cat used to going in a carrier, keep the carrier open and in a place that he can access and use as a refuge. If he regards the carrier as a place of safety, he will be happier to travel in it - even if it results in a trip to the vet.

Cat carrier

CARRIER CRITERIA
A good cat carrier will be easy to enter and exit. It will shield your cat from the outside but still let in plenty of fresh air and light, and allow him to see out.

Collar

COLLARS AND TAGS
A collar is a must for an outdoor cat. Your ID can be engraved on a disc or sealed in a cylinder pendant. A bell will protect birds by warning of your cat's approach.

Disc tag   **Cylinder tag**   **Bell**

Cat cage

CAGE OPTION
An open cage may be more suitable if your cat doesn't like the confines of a carrier. While a carrier will fit neatly on a car seat, a cage may have to be put securely in the back of a large car.

A new family member

FIRST DAYS

Moving to a new home can be as strange an experience for a new cat or kitten as it is for a human. Although a cat will quickly adapt to his new surroundings, you should aim to make his first few days in an unfamiliar household as calm and stress-free as possible. To aid this, some advance planning and a course of action discussed with the entire family will help him to feel at ease.

Thinking ahead

Plan to bring your cat home on a day when your house will be very calm and quiet, so that you can devote all your attention to him. If you have children, explain to them that their new pet will be a little scared at first and that they should give him time to get used to them. Don't let them get overexcited about this fresh addition to the family. If you've never had a family pet before, try to make your children understand that the cat is not a toy and will need to be kept calm for the first few days.

Transporting your cat

Your cat or kitten needs a secure box or cat carrier to be transported safely. If possible, put a piece of his bedding into the carrier so that he recognizes the familiar smell. Cover the carrier if necessary so that he can only see out of one end; this will help to reduce his anxiety. Strap the carrier into the car seat with a safety belt or place it in a footwell to prevent your cat from being flung about if you have to stop suddenly.

TOP TIP

Some cats are bolder than others. If your cat leaves the carrier quickly and appears confident, try introducing a toy and playing with him for a while. This will help to break the ice and make your cat feel more relaxed in his new home.

FIRST STEPS

A cat will feel more in control if you let him emerge when he wants. If you force him out, you will merely succeed in causing anxiety.

Welcome home

When you arrive back at your house, bring your cat into the room where he will be spending his first few days. It's best to restrict him to one or two rooms until he is settled. Check that any doors and windows are closed. If you already have other pets, make sure they are out of the way in another room. Put the carrier on the floor and open the door. Allow your cat to venture out in his own time; be patient, and do not try to remove him yourself. Curiosity will eventually get the better of him, and he will leave the carrier and start to explore.

Showing your cat the ropes

Part of your cat's acclimatization involves introducing him to the essential elements of his new life: his basket, the litter tray, feeding station, and scratching post. Make sure that these are in easily accessible places but are away from busy areas of the house. It is best to start with the litter tray - with any luck your cat will use it straight away. If the tray is in a separate room, make sure that he can always get to it. Feeding bowls should be put in a place where it is easy to clean up any spills.

Meeting the residents

It will be hard to keep small children away from something as exciting and cute as a new cat or kitten. However, too much shouting, shrieking, and rushing around may frighten your cat, so make sure they understand this. Show them how to hold your cat correctly (p.216) and let them stroke or cuddle him, but if he starts looking unhappy, then be swift to intervene and take control - a nasty scratch could put a child off their new pet for a long while. Perhaps think about providing children with an activity or treat that will keep them out of the way for an hour or two after they have been introduced to their new pet, so as not to overwhelm him. Also, make them aware that what they leave on the floor could be dangerous to their new kitten - such as small toys - and that they will need to look where they're going from now on to avoid treading on him.

WHAT'S MY NAME?

Think carefully about what you are going to call your cat. Cats respond best to short, one- or two-syllable names. Make sure it sounds different from the names of any other pets or even members of the family, so that he will learn to recognize his own name and come when called.

INTRODUCTIONS
When showing a new cat to a child, always keep hold of him. Children need to learn how to handle a pet, so let them follow your example.

Start as you mean to go on

Establish the ground rules from the outset, especially about feeding and sleeping. If you give your cat morsels from your plate, for example, he will always expect titbits and may even refuse his own food. Make sure everyone in the house knows and sticks to the rules. A cat will not understand if you allow him to do something one day but not the next.

BEDTIME RULES
If you allow your new cat to sleep on your bed at night, that is where he will always expect to sleep in the future.

READY FOR A NEW HOME
Kittens are used to the warmth and companionship of littermates and may be timid on their own. Given love and patience, your new cat will soon become a confident member of the family.

Establishing a routine

Cats are creatures of habit. Setting a routine in the early days will help your cat or kitten to settle into his new home and make him feel secure. Eventually, your cat will develop his own patterns of behaviour around your family's daily schedule.

Base your routine around regular activities such as feeding, grooming, and playtime. You will need to be consistent with this for several months, so make sure it fits in with your own commitments and habits. Cats are not keen on constant change – it can stress them and may result in behavioural problems such as digging, chewing, biting, and general hostility. A regular routine will also help you notice any changes in your cat's behaviour and health. Predictability means safety to your cat.

Decide on regular mealtimes for your cat, and always put the bowls in the same place. By doing this, you can keep an eye on his appetite, and it will also prove useful for training to know when he's hungry.

If your cat needs regular grooming, aim to do this at the same time each day. Grooming may not be your cat's favourite activity, but it will be tolerated if your pet knows it's only going to take a limited amount of time. Grooming just before feeding or playtime will give your cat an incentive to be near at hand and to cooperate with the process.

Having a regular playtime is also a good idea. It gives your cat something to look forward to and reduces the likelihood of "mad hours", when your cat goes crazy and rushes about the house or won't leave you alone. Make sure that playtime is a worthwhile experience with plenty of variety and a decent amount of time devoted solely to the cat.

TOP TIP

Plan through when you will give your cat his first feed. You won't want your cat howling for its 6 a.m. weekday breakfast on a Saturday or Sunday if you like having a weekend lie-in. If you train a cat to eat at a certain time, stick to your side of the bargain – feed him at the same time every day.

REGULAR MEALTIMES
Giving your cat meals at set times of the day is just one of many routines that will help him to adjust to his new home.

PREPARING THE LITTER TRAY
Make sure the litter tray is set up and ready for use by the time you bring your cat home – you never know how soon it may be needed.

TRAY SHARING
The general rule is one litter tray per cat, but if you start them young they may accept a shared tray.

TOXOPLASMOSIS

Cat faeces may contain the parasite *Toxoplasma gondii*. Humans can be infected by *T. gondii* from contact with cat faeces, contaminated soil, and cat litter. The infection, called toxoplasmosis, may produce a flu-like reaction, but in most cases there are no symptoms at all. However, it is dangerous for pregnant women to come into contact with cat faeces, because the infection can be passed to the unborn baby. In extreme cases, this can result in problems as serious as blindness and brain damage.

Litter-tray etiquette

Most cats and kittens will already know how to use a litter tray by the time you bring them home, but an unfamiliar tray or litter product may cause a few problems in the early stages. A cat used to one type of litter may not like changing to another. Use the same litter as the breeder initially, so the cat first has a chance to get used to the tray. Then you can make the change to the new product gradually, by mixing the two types, adding a greater proportion of the new product each time you change the litter.

If your cat is avoiding the litter tray, try setting up another tray containing a different product to see which he prefers. Generally, the finer the product feels under his paws, the more attractive it will be to a cat, which is why most instinctively go for sand or earth. Keep the litter tray in the same place all the time and within easy access. If the location is too busy, your cat may refuse to use his tray – cats like their privacy too. Clean the tray out regularly. Scoop out clumps every day and change the litter once a week. Rinse the tray well after washing to remove any lingering chemical smell, and resist the temptation to mask litter odours with scented sanitizers or deodorants.

Coping with change

There will always be times when routines have to change. Some changes can be positive experiences for your cat, so long as they don't make him feel threatened or stressed. There will inevitably be occasions when you have to go out for the day and leave your cat on his own, which will disrupt his usual playtime or grooming sessions. It won't matter if you have these sessions before you go out or when you come back instead, or even abandon them completely, but do try to make a fuss of your cat at some point and leave him with toys so that he can entertain himself.

Going on holiday

Holidays are always tricky times for cat owners, and you will need to organize things so that your cat's routine remains as constant as possible. Cats can adjust to their owner being away or being taken to a new place, but rarely to the two happening at the same time. The best option is to ask a friend or relative to come in and feed your cat at home. If this is not possible and you have to resort to professional pet sitters, then make sure you ask for references.

Catteries can be stressful places for cats, so it's vital to choose a good one. Ask cat owners whose judgement you trust if they can recommend any. Go and visit a cattery before using it, to see conditions for yourself. They should have a licence from a suitable authority – don't be afraid to ask to see it. Remember to book well in advance, especially if the cattery is popular.

HOLIDAY HOME
A good cattery will have separate sleeping and exercise areas for each cat, without allowing contact between the animals.

FOOD AND FEEDING

A well-fed and well-nourished cat is a happy cat. Although the occasional mouse caught outside may supplement your cat's diet, he will rely on you almost exclusively for his food. And that reliance places great responsibility on you. Providing your cat with a healthy, balanced diet will help him to grow and develop as he should, and give him the best chance of living a long life free of illness.

Eating healthily for a long life

Essential nutrition

Cats are carnivores – they eat meat because they cannot convert the fats and proteins found in vegetable matter into the amino acids and fatty acids necessary for their bodies to function properly and stay healthy. Meat protein contains everything they need plus an important amino acid that they cannot make – taurine. Insufficient taurine in a cat's diet can lead to blindness and heart disease. Taurine is added to all processed cat foods. It is impaired by cooking, so if you cook your cat's food yourself, you will also need to provide him with a regular taurine supplement.

Vitamins and micronutrients

The vitamins needed for essential cat nutrition include D, K, E, B, and A (cats cannot manufacture vitamin A). They also need vitamin C, but intake of this vitamin should be monitored, as cats can develop bladder stones if they have too much. Cats also require certain micronutrients – for example, phosphorus, selenium, and sodium. Although these are only needed in tiny quantities, a lack of them can lead to serious health problems. A source of calcium is vital too as calcium only occurs in small quantities in meat. Most commercial cat food contains all of these essential vitamins and micronutrients.

Wet or dry?

Most prepared cat food is described as "wet" or "dry". Wet food comes in airtight tins or pouches, so it doesn't need preservatives to keep it fresh. It is tasty but soft in texture, so it provides little resistance to keep teeth and gums healthy. If wet food is not eaten immediately, it will soon become unappealing to your cat.

Dry food has been pressure-cooked and then dried. It is sprayed with fat to make it palatable, but this requires preservatives to be added. Dry foods usually includes antioxidants such as vitamin C and E, which are natural and beneficial to your cat. Although you shouldn't give your cat dry food all the

FIBRE FROM PREY
Cats require a source of fibre to maintain healthy gut and bowel function. In the wild, they obtain the fibre they need from the fur, skin, and feathers of their prey.

Dry food

Wet food

Home-cooked

WET, DRY, AND HOME-COOKED FOOD
Dry food won't spoil, but wet food is more like a cat's natural diet. Home-made meals are freshest, but avoid single-protein diets.

time, it does have some advantages. It can, for example, be left out during the day without spoiling. You may want to give dry food in the morning and reserve the wet food for when you return from work in the evening.

Home-cooked food

For home-cooked meals, use meat and fish that's fit for human consumption. Make sure it is well cooked to kill bacteria or parasites that could be dangerous. Home-made meals are a good way of introducing well-cooked bones as a calcium source, but don't offer them if your cat has not learned to eat bones or if he eats his food too quickly. The scraping action of bones keeps teeth in good shape; without them, your cat's teeth will need regular cleaning (p.231).

Drinking requirements

All cats should be provided with a source of water, since water helps dilute the urine and is absorbed by fibre in the gut. Caution should be taken with giving cats milk or cream, since many adult cats lack the enzyme necessary to digest the lactose sugar in dairy products and may get diarrhoea. Special "cat milk" can now be bought; alternatively, use milk for lactose-intolerant humans available at supermarkets.

Foods to avoid

As well as milk and cream, other foods to avoid include raw fish, which contains enzymes that can be harmful to cats. Onions and garlic can cause anaemia, while green tomatoes and green (raw) potatoes – and especially their leaves – contain a poisonous alkaloid that produces violent gastrointestinal symptoms so keep these items out of reach. Chocolate is highly toxic to cats, and grapes and raisins may harm the kidneys.

DRINKING WATER
Cats fed a dry-food diet will require more water than those that eat wet food.

DANGEROUS FOODS

Onions and garlic

Green tomatoes and potatoes

Chocolate

Grapes and raisins

Cream

Raw fish

When and how much to feed

Generally, your cat should be fed twice a day at regular times. This will allow him to build up an appetite and you to regulate how much he eats. Once you have established a regular feeding regime, it will be easy to tell if your cat is off his food and unwell. The feeding guides printed on packets of

CAT GRASS

Cats eat grass because its juices contain folic acid, which prevents anaemia. Cat grass bought from a pet store or nursery can be grown indoors in a small pot.

EATING THE RIGHT AMOUNT

If you have more than one kitten, make sure that they are all eating the right quantity for their age and weight. If you suspect one isn't eating enough, try feeding him separately so that you can monitor his intake.

prepared food are only estimates, and they may need to be increased or decreased depending on how your cat looks and feels when handled. As a guideline, you should be able to feel your cat's ribs easily but not see them. Make sure you never feed an adult cat kitten food or dog food – kitten food contains too much protein and will be bad for an adult cat's kidneys; conversely, dog food does not contain enough protein for a cat. Make sure your cat's food and water bowls are always washed thoroughly after use.

The right balance

Cats enjoy variety, and it is important that they are fed a mix of different foodstuffs to ensure they get adequate nutrition. Make any changes to your cat's diet gradually, so that he can build up enough bacteria in his gut to digest the new food. Once you've found a balanced diet that your cat likes, stick to it. Constantly changing his food may encourage him to become a fussy eater and cats can hold out for days until you give them what they want.

Special diets

Your cat's dietary needs will change throughout his life. Kittens need lots of protein, fat, and calories to support their rapid growth. Use specially formulated kitten food to avoid deficiencies that could cause problems later in life. For the first week after bringing your kitten home, give him the same food that he has eaten since weaning. To introduce a new foodstuff, replace 10 per cent of the original food with the new food, increasing the proportion by 10 per cent daily until your kitten is eating only the new food by the tenth day – this will prevent diarrhoea. If he does get an upset stomach, revert to a higher proportion of the old food and take longer to make the switch-over.

A pregnant cat needs extra protein and vitamins, and will want to eat more in the final stages of pregnancy. This may mean giving her smaller meals more frequently if she cannot eat as much as usual in one go. She will also have increased nutritional requirements when nursing. Older cats use less energy, so they need fewer calories in their diet. They may need special food to aid a more delicate digestive system.

For cats with medical conditions and overweight cats, use a diet recommended by your vet. An approved weight-loss diet ensures that an obese cat loses weight but stays nourished and still eats a satisfying volume of food. Food allergies in cats are rare, but when they occur the only way to find the cause is through a food-elimination trial supervised by your vet.

The role of treats

Whether given as rewards in training or to aid bonding with your cat, try to ration treats to avoid your cat gaining weight. Ensure that 10 per cent maximum of your cat's calorie intake comes from treats. Some treats may give nutritional benefits that your cat won't get from his normal food; others contain "filler" ingredients with little nutritional value and lots of fat. Learn to distinguish good ingredients from bad.

IT'S TREAT TIME
Rewards for learning new tricks will reinforce training, while treats given when you leave for work and return home can be something your pet looks forward to.

WHICH TREAT?
Treats come in many different meat and fish flavours. Whatever you choose, make sure you don't overfeed your cat.

FEEDING YOUR CAT						
ADULT WEIGHT		2KG	4KG	6KG	10KG	12KG
Inactive lifestyle		100-140kcal (120g wet/30g dry)	200-280kcal (240g wet/60g dry)	300-420kcal (360g wet/90g dry)	400-560kcal (480g wet/120g dry)	500-700kcal (600g wet/150g dry)
Active lifestyle		140-180kcal (160g wet/40g dry)	280-360kcal (320g wet/80g dry)	420-540kcal (480g wet/120g dry)	560-720kcal (640g wet/160g dry)	700-900kcal (800g wet/200g dry)
Pregnant female		200-280kcal (240g wet/60g dry)	400-560kcal (480g wet/120g dry)	600-840kcal (720g wet/180g dry)	800-1120kcal (960g wet/240g dry)	1,000-1,400kcal (1,200g wet/300g dry)

HANDLING YOUR CAT

Cats are notoriously choosy about who they will allow to touch them, let alone pick them up and pet them. Some cats simply don't like being picked up and will struggle to get free. There are right and wrong ways to handle a cat – learn how to do it properly and your cat will enjoy the opportunity to get closer to you. If he's comfortable with being held, it will be easier for you to groom him and check for injury or illness.

A correctly held kitten

STRESS-BUSTER
There's something about cats that makes us want to stroke them. Research has shown that petting cats is good for reducing stress in humans – and cats like it too.

Start early

The best time to get a cat used to being handled is when it is a kitten. Early and routine contact from about two or three weeks old helps kittens not only to develop faster but also grow into more contented cats that are happy to be handled by humans. If you have children, teach them to be gentle and to treat the kitten with respect. Mistreated and mishandled kittens will grow into nervous cats who keep their distance from people and who are difficult to train. Cats have long memories, and they will avoid children who handle them too roughly or pull their tails.

How to pick up a cat

A very young kitten can be picked up by the scruff of his neck, like his mother does, but he will need more support as he gets older and heavier. When his mother stops picking him up like this, so should you. From then on, the correct way to pick up your cat will be to approach from the side and place one hand flat against his ribcage, just behind his front legs. Use the other hand to support him under his hindquarters.

CARRYING YOUR CAT
Don't cradle your cat on its back when you pick him up – this position is unnatural to a cat and will make him feel vulnerable. Instead, try to hold him as upright as possible. Put one hand under the "armpits" of his front legs, place the other under his rear, and hold him securely.

Different strokes

Try not to stroke your cat unless he is willing to be touched. Put out a hand or finger for him to sniff. If he touches you with his nose or rubs his cheek or body against you, he's in the mood for contact. If he shows no interest, leave it until another time.

Once your cat is amenable to being petted, begin by stroking him along his back in a slow, continuous motion. Always go from head to tail, never the other way. Stop when you reach his tail. If your cat is enjoying it, he may arch his back to increase the pressure of your hand.

Learn how your cat likes to be petted. The top of the head, especially between and behind the ears, is often a favourite place. Cats can't reach this spot, and it reminds them of when their mother used to lick them there. Some cats also like being stroked under the chin. Rubbing the cheeks with a circular motion is popular with many cats, because it helps them spread their scent on to your fingers.

HEAD SCRATCHING
Scratch with the pads of your fingers from back to front. Be slow and gentle – cats can be fussy about how they are stroked.

Your cat may like being raked with the fingers, but don't stop and scratch him in one place. Most cats dislike being patted, especially along the flank. When your cat jumps into your lap and lies down, pet him once to see if he wants attention or just a warm place to snooze. If he fidgets or his tail twitches, stop stroking. A cat that is enjoying being petted may change his position so that the part he wants stroking is uppermost and closest to your hand.

Rough and tumble

Some cats like rough play and will grab and "play bite" at a hand that tries to rub their belly. If your cat sinks his claws in, keep still until he disengages. Pushing further in towards him may surprise him enough to let go. In general, when you stop, so will he. If he kicks with his back legs at your hand, don't assume that he wants his paws touched. Try stroking one foot lightly with a finger in the direction of his fur; if he pulls his foot away, flattens his ears, or walks off, let him be.

Knowing when to stop

Watch your cat's body language and stop stroking if he seems to be getting angry (pp.224-5). Be careful if he is on his back exposing his belly, as this is not necessarily an invitation to pet; it may be an aggressive defence posture that leaves him free to kick, bite, or claw. If you misjudge his mood and get a bite or a scratch that breaks the skin, wash the wound and treat it with antiseptic. See your doctor if the area around the bite swells and starts weeping.

CAT MAKING CONTACT
Your cat may often make the first move himself, by bumping or brushing up against you. If it's not convenient for you to pet him, at least stroke your cat once or twice so he knows he's not being ignored.

SOCIALIZING YOUR CAT

**Dogs and cats
need not be arch enemies**

By nature, cats are solitary creatures. That said, some cats are able to live quite happily in groups. Bringing a new cat into your home may change his whole outlook on the people and other animals around him. But if introductions are made carefully and sensitively, your cat will grow into a confident, friendly animal that can cope with all social situations.

Start early

Socialization should start in kittenhood. Give your kitten plenty of opportunities to meet new people, cats, and dogs, and make it a fun and rewarding experience. Introduce him to friends, neighbours, and the vet at an early stage; keep initial encounters brief and reward your kitten with treats for good behaviour. A cat that is not exposed to new situations as a kitten may grow up to be timid and fearful, and liable to react badly to being touched or approached by strangers.

Kittens start to learn social skills from their mother between 8 and 12 weeks of age. Be wary of bringing home a kitten younger than this, otherwise his socialization will be your responsibility. It is important that your kitten gets used to being handled, with plenty of play designed to hone his predatory skills, but let him sleep when he wants to. Kittens left to spend a long time on their own without stimulation or attention may develop antisocial behaviours and grow up to be aloof or aggressive towards people and other animals.

Socializing an adult cat

Adult cats take longer than kittens to adapt to new people and surroundings. Changes in routine are upsetting for an older cat, and unless you are familiar with your cat's previous home there may be issues related to how he has

OLDER AND CALMER
If you have very small children, it may be better to get an adult cat. Toddlers may not realize how gently they need to handle a kitten, whereas an older cat may be more tolerant of children.

been treated in the past. Try to get as much information as possible from the previous owner or rescue centre about the cat's personality, habits, motivations, and favourite food and toys. Familiar objects can also help him to settle in, so try to bring some of his old bedding or toys to make him feel more secure. Provide him with a refuge, such as a carrier or box, to which he can retreat and feel safe when things get too much.

An older cat may initially be wary of contact with his new owners and may resist being touched. Let him explore his surroundings in his own time. Talk to him in a low, soothing tone so that he gets used to your presence and the sound of your voice. Gradually accustom him to being handled by rewarding him with treats. One of the chief problems with poorly socialized cats is that they play too rough, biting and

SOCIALIZING MOTHER
Adopting a kitten less than 12 weeks old is not often recommended, as it still needs a lot of socialization time with its mother, who will teach it essential life skills.

scratching to get what they want. If that is the case, simply stop playing with him, say "no" in a firm voice, and give him a toy instead. If your cat learns that biting or scratching achieves the outcome he wants, it will be difficult to get him to break the habit. Give plenty of praise when your cat is playing nicely with you, but also praise him when he takes his aggression out on a toy. That way, he will learn that he can play hard with toys but not with you.

New people need to be introduced with care. Never force your cat to meet strangers. Instead, let him approach the person when he is ready; once he realizes that nothing bad is going to happen, he will be more confident and trusting. You can speed up the process by laying a trail of treats up to the stranger. This works best when your cat is hungry. (You can also restrict treats to occasions when there is a visitor in the house.) When your cat is comfortable with the person, a friendly stroke or two on the head or back can be attempted. If you have to leave your cat to be looked after by friends or neighbours, get him used to the new people in advance. Ask them to come to your home frequently to feed him treats and pet or play with him. He will soon look forward to their visits.

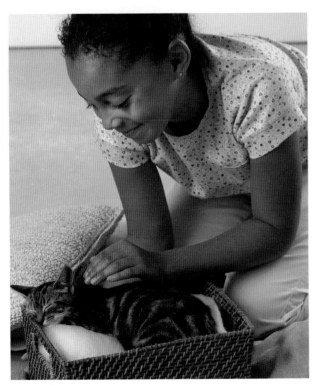

GETTING USED TO CHILDREN
A new cat will be an irresistible attraction to any children in your family. Teach them the correct way to approach and handle a cat, and make sure you supervise their initial encounters.

Introducing children

If you have small children, your cat may feel threatened and frightened by their exuberant, noisy behaviour and sudden movements – especially if they chase him. His preferred defence will be to run away, but when cornered he may respond by hissing, scratching, or biting, all of which may scare or hurt a small child. It pays to prepare your children for the cat's arrival by reading through a book about cat care with them. First meetings should be supervised, especially if toddlers are involved. Let your cat or kitten take the initiative and approach the child. If he decides to flee, let him go. Play sessions should involve the child sitting still on the floor with a lure toy or ribbon that encourages the cat to come closer.

To make your children feel involved, give each responsibility for some aspect of the cat's care, such as filling the water bowl, shaking out the bedding, putting his food away, or collecting his toys. To avoid overfeeding, make sure only one child has the job of feeding your cat. Never let a young child clean out your cat's litter tray. Cat faeces can carry intestinal parasites, such as worms, and an infection called toxoplasmosis that can be harmful to a young child (p.211).

A new baby

If your cat has always been the centre of attention, he may become jealous of the competition for affection when a new baby arrives. Some careful preparation can help prevent this. Before the birth, allow your cat to examine the baby's room and equipment, but make it clear that he is not allowed in on his own and that the cot, baby basket, and pram are distinctly off limits. If you have friends or family with a baby, ask them to visit so that your cat becomes familiar with the sounds and smells. To accommodate the new domestic situation, you may need to change your cat's routine or how much time you will be spending with him. Introduce such changes gradually in the months leading up to the birth. Likewise, if your cat has any behavioural problems that you need to put right, now is the time to do it, since they may get worse when the baby arrives.

A NEW COMPANION
The arrival of a new baby need cause no problems for your cat if you get him used to the idea well in advance of the birth.

When you bring the baby home for the first time, allow your cat to sit next to the baby and give him treats for good behaviour so that he associates the baby with a positive experience. Never leave the baby and cat alone together. Close the door to the room where your baby is sleeping or buy a screen to cover the door frame. You can also get nets to put over cots and prams, which will deter your cat from trying to snuggle up to your baby or from spraying if he is stressed. Try to keep your cat's routine as normal as possible and make sure he gets his share of attention from someone in the family.

Cats and dogs

Whether you are introducing a new cat to a dog or a new dog to a cat, the same methods of socializing them can be used, with slight modification. When you first bring your new cat home, put him in a room that the dog does not need to access until the cat has settled in. Alternatively, put up a barrier or put the dog in a crate. While the cat is getting used to his new surroundings, let the dog smell the cat's scent. You can do this by rubbing the dog with a towel that you have previously rubbed on the cat or letting the dog sniff your hands after handling the cat. Do the same with the cat. Once the dog is familiar with the cat's scent, put the dog on a lead and bring him to the door of the cat's room. Do not allow any bad behaviour such as barking, scratching, or lunging. If the dog behaves properly, try letting him off the lead.

For the next stage of socialization, allow the dog through the door while on the lead, or put him in a crate in the cat's room. Let the pair sniff each other, but remove the dog if he attempts to jump on or chase the cat. Supervise encounters until the cat is comfortable around the dog. Initial contacts should be short and repeated several times a day. Praise and reward the dog for good behaviour, so that he comes to regard the cat's presence in the house as a good thing.

Finally, you can try leaving the two alone in the room by walking out then walking back in straight away. Gradually extend the period of leaving them alone, but stay within listening distance. If you hear hissing, growling, or barking, return immediately. Make sure the cat has a safe place to hide that is out of the dog's reach. Continue this process until the dog no longer reacts to the cat, and the cat is happy to eat or sleep when the dog is in the same room. Sadly, some dogs may never be safe to leave with a cat. If that is the case, you will have to keep them separate or supervise their encounters at all times.

Other cats in the home

Because your cat sees your home as his territory, bringing another adult cat into the house may be seen as a threat. A new kitten, however, is more likely to be tolerated by the resident. Keep a lookout for bullying and jealousy on the part of the adult cat. If it looks like the older cat is picking on the kitten, keep the two apart until the newcomer is more able to look after itself. Remember, this is the older cat's territory and his natural instinct is to protect it from interlopers, however small. Make sure that the older cat gets his share of love and attention, and reward him with treats for good behaviour. The two will gradually get used to each other and develop a companionable truce.

ACCEPTING ADULT
Adding a new kitten into the household does not usually threaten an adult cat's dominance. The older cat will most likely tolerate the kitten, understanding its playfulness to be part of its natural behaviour.

LEARNING TO BE FRIENDS

Cats and dogs are not natural allies, but they can learn to get on. The dog must understand that the cat is not prey. Make sure the dog does not get overexcited, so the cat will feel safe when he is around.

INDOORS OR OUTDOORS?

One of the most important decisions you need to make before you acquire a cat is whether it is going to be a house cat or left free to roam the great outdoors. For many people, the decision rests on how "great" the outdoors would be for their cat. Owners need to take stock of their own lifestyle and their home's surroundings when deciding what is best for the long-term safety and happiness of their cat.

The freedom of the catflap

Call of the wild

Domestic cats were once wild animals, adapted to living in open spaces. Many of their wild instincts remain, but the world that cats inhabit has changed dramatically. Many cat owners live in urban environments, surrounded by busy roads, buildings, people, and other animals, and an outdoor cat will have to contend with all these hazards. In making your indoors-or-outdoors decision, the safety of your cat is paramount. Not all cats develop a good road sense, and some fall victim to passing cars. If you let your cat out at night, buy it a collar with reflective patches that can be seen in the dark by drivers. Cats are naturally more active at dawn or dusk – times that often correspond with rush hours. Try to keep your cat indoors at these times. Given the run of the neighbourhood, your cat will probably explore beyond your garden, leading to encounters with other neighbourhood cats, and possibly wild animals too.

WINDOW ON THE WORLD
If your cat is to be truly independent, install a catflap so that he can come and go as he pleases. Otherwise, you will be perpetually opening doors and windows to see whether he wants to go out.

Creating cat heaven

The best way to keep an outdoor cat close to home is to make your garden a cat-friendly sanctuary. Plant it with bushes to provide shade and shelter and a few scented plants that cats love – such as catnip, mint, valerian, heather, and lemongrass – in sunny places for your cat to bask among. A clump of cat grass is ideal for your pet to snack on if you habitually spray your grass and plants with chemicals.

A PLACE IN THE SUN
Provide your cat with plenty of spots in the garden to bask and doze. A garden trug makes an ideal bed for a laid-back cat.

Territorial disputes

Once your garden is cat-friendly, it will undoubtedly attract other cats. Feline disputes are certain to break out, because cats are territorial animals. Make sure your cat is neutered – especially if she is female – to prevent unwanted pregnancies. Neutered cats need smaller territories, but that won't stop your cat from straying or an unneutered feral tomcat from invading your cat's territory and picking a fight. Make sure that your cat is immunized against all diseases, because fights will inevitably lead to bites and scratches.

Keeping in with the neighbours

Appreciate that not all of your neighbours are cat lovers. Some people are allergic to cats and go to great lengths to avoid them. Even the best-trained cats have bad habits – they dig up flowerbeds to defecate, chew on plants, spray, rip open rubbish bags, chase birds, and wander into other houses uninvited. If your cat has been neutered, tell your neighbour that neutered cats bury their droppings and that their urine is less smelly. You can always provide them with a water pistol to squirt at the cat if they really want to deter it.

Indoor cats

Your cat will live a longer and healthier life if it stays indoors – but it will be your responsibility to keep it happy. If you are out at work all day, your cat will need a regular playtime or, better still, a companion. Bored cats grow frustrated and stressed, and can become overweight and unhealthy if they aren't exercised. Stress may manifest itself in scratching and biting or urinating outside the litter tray. Despite their natural instincts, cats kept indoors from birth will rarely want to venture out, because they see your home as their territory. Once they get a taste for going out, however,

KEEPING A CLOSE WATCH
Cats like to take up elevated positions from which they can watch over their territory. Shed roofs, fences, and pedestals – ideally in different parts of the garden – are perfect for this.

they may want to do it more and more and look for any chance to escape. If so, you will have to be vigilant about closing windows and doors. Be extra careful in a high-rise apartment – many cats have died after falling from an open window or jumping over a balcony while chasing birds or insects.

Indoor cats need space to exercise, so they should have access to several rooms, especially if you have more than one cat – like us, cats need their own "personal space". To give your cat a breath of fresh air you could screen off a porch, patio, or balcony that he can access through a catflap. Even if you live in a block of flats, consider allowing your cat out into the hallway for a game that will allow him to run around. Ensure that any doors leading to the outside are closed first.

GOOD COMPANY
If they are not siblings, companion cats are best introduced early in their lives. They will provide company and a playmate for each other if you are out at work all day.

TOP TIPS

■ **With indoor cats,** you should always check where your cat is before leaving him alone in the house. Make especially sure you do not accidentally shut him away in a confined area such as a wardrobe or cupboard.

■ **If you have** an outdoor cat, attach a bell to his collar to warn the wildlife in your garden of his presence. Bird tables and scattered food are a magnet for cats, so avoid leaving food out and keep bird feeders well out of reach of predatory cats.

CAT COMMUNICATION

You can always tell when a dog is happy or sad - its emotions are written all over its face. You will find your cat more inscrutable when it comes to facial expressions, so it may be difficult to know what your cat is trying to tell you. Cats do, however, have a whole range of other behaviours and signals that you can learn to interpret, which will make for much easier interaction between you and your cat.

Learn to understand your cat

How to speak cat

Wild cats are solitary, predatory animals that patrol a territory they regard as exclusively theirs. Consequently, most cat communications are designed to ward off intruders. Learning what your cat's body language, and the noises he makes, mean will help you understand what he is trying to tell you.

Chief among cat noises are hissing, growling, miaowing, and purring. Hisses and growls - sometimes accompanied by a flash of teeth or show of claws - are warnings to usurpers trespassing on the cat's territory or to humans who get too close. Miaows - rarely used between adult cats - are mainly a way for kittens to signal to their mother. Domestically, your cat will use miaowing to announce his presence. Short and high-pitched chirps and squeaks usually signal excitement or a plea for something, but drawn-out and low-pitched sounds express displeasure or a demand. Rapid, intense, and loud repeated sounds often signify anxiety. Long, drawn-out cries and shrieks indicate that the cat is in pain or fighting. Mating cats produce long wails known as caterwauls. Purring is usually a sound of contentment, but cats also purr as a way of comforting themselves when they are in pain or anxious.

Body language

Your cat will give you signals using his ears, tail, whiskers, and eyes. Ears and whiskers usually work together. Normally the ears are erect and facing forward and the whiskers are to the front or sides, showing that your cat is alert and interested. When his ears are rotated back and flat and his whiskers are forward, he is feeling aggressive. Ears out to the sides and whiskers flat against the cheeks mean that your cat is scared.

Cats don't like eye contact, which is why your cat will often make for anyone in the room who ignores him: to him, this is friendly behaviour. Once your cat is used to those around him, he will find eye contact less threatening. Dilated pupils can mean he is interested and excited or fearful and aggressive, so always try to read the other signals he is giving out too.

INTIMIDATING EYE CONTACT
Cats use eye contact as a form of intimidation to avoid a fight. Staring is perceived as a threat, and two cats will try to out-stare each other until one looks away or slinks off.

TOP TIPS

Speak cat, not human. If you hiss or make a spitting noise when you say "no" to unacceptable behaviour, your cat will understand that it is doing something wrong. This will prove much more effective than shouting at him.

TAIL SIGNALS

The most obvious signs of your cat's mood are the visual signals he sends out. Although he will give you signals with all parts of his body, one of the best barometers of his emotional state is his tail. When you look at your cat, the way he is carrying and moving his tail will be a clear expression of the way he is currently feeling. Try to learn these different tail configurations and their meanings. Remember that his mood can change in an instant.

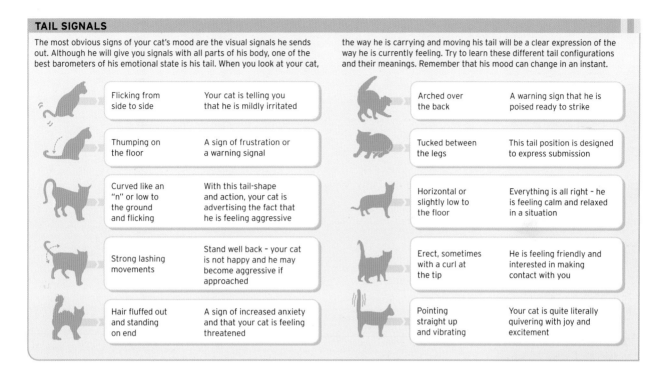

Flicking from side to side	Your cat is telling you that he is mildly irritated
Thumping on the floor	A sign of frustration or a warning signal
Curved like an "n" or low to the ground and flicking	With this tail-shape and action, your cat is advertising the fact that he is feeling aggressive
Strong lashing movements	Stand well back – your cat is not happy and he may become aggressive if approached
Hair fluffed out and standing on end	A sign of increased anxiety and that your cat is feeling threatened

Arched over the back	A warning sign that he is poised ready to strike
Tucked between the legs	This tail position is designed to express submission
Horizontal or slightly low to the floor	Everything is all right – he is feeling calm and relaxed in a situation
Erect, sometimes with a curl at the tip	He is feeling friendly and interested in making contact with you
Pointing straight up and vibrating	Your cat is quite literally quivering with joy and excitement

Posture

Your cat's posture tells you one of two things: "go away" or "come closer". Lying, sitting in a relaxed manner, or coming towards you indicates that he is approachable. A cat on his back exposing his belly is not being submissive like a dog: this is usually a fight posture that allows him to wield all his claws and teeth. However, if he is also rolling from side to side, you can assume that he is in a playful mood. Avoid touching his belly too much or you may get scratched or bitten. Wiggling the rump is another sign that he is up for a play. When your cat is crouching – either looking sideways or with his tail wrapped around his body – he is looking for a chance to escape, pounce, or go on the offensive.

WARNING STANCE
When your cat stands with rump raised or back arched, he is feeling threatened and warning that he is about to attack. The hair on his body may also be raised.

CAT SPRAYING
Spraying is a perfectly natural behaviour, and you should not punish your cat for doing it.

Smell and touch

Cats have a superb sense of smell, so they use urine and scent to mark territory and leave messages for other cats. A cat that is not neutered will spray to warn

of his presence, threaten any rivals, and announce that he is ready to mate. If a neutered cat still sprays, he is probably feeling anxious. Investigate what is triggering this behaviour.

Cats also spread scent from glands on their cheeks, paws, and tail by rubbing them on surfaces or other cats. These scents mark territory and form social bonds. Cats that live together will rub each other along the flanks or the head, creating a group scent that alerts them to the presence of strangers. Your cat will also rub the members of your family to mark you all as part of his "gang". Cats sniff nose-to-nose when they meet; unfamiliar cats end the encounter there, but friendly cats progress to rubbing heads or licking each other's face or ears. Scratching is another way of leaving scent, as well as being a visual signal of a cat's presence.

THE IMPORTANCE OF PLAY

Playful kitten

No matter how pampered their existence, cats need some excitement in their lives. A cat deprived of opportunities to hunt and stalk becomes bored and stressed. This is a real problem with indoor cats, often locked up alone in a house all day. Yet, with forethought and commitment on your part, your cat can have an interesting and fun home life.

Going on instinct

Kept indoors alone all day, a bored cat will constantly pester you for attention when you get home. Outdoor cats have a riskier but happier and more active lifestyle. With plenty of fresh air, space to run and jump around, and exposure to new experiences, they can give free rein to their natural instincts for exploring, chasing, and hunting. Even when indoors a cat will need to let off steam regularly. Often, this takes the form of a "mad moment", when the cat rushes around the room, leaping on to furniture and climbing the curtains before bolting off. This is perfectly natural behaviour, but uncontrolled sessions like this run the risk of damaging your home and causing injury to your cat.

BORN FREE
A cat that cannot follow its instincts may become troublesome.

CONSTRUCTIVE PLAY | CHANNEL THE ENERGY

CHASING AND PLAYING
To prevent manic bursts of activity, channel your kitten's predatory instincts into constructive play. Dangling or dragging along a piece of ribbon will appeal to your kitten's natural urge to hunt and stalk.

CATCHING AND BITING
Play also helps your kitten learn essential skills for survival in the wild, such as catching and biting prey. Most cats, especially if neutered, will still retain their sense of playfulness as they get older.

Furry mouse

Fabric mouse with bell

Play balls

Feather

TOY PARADE
There is a wide range of playthings available for cats, from balls and pretend mice to catnip-scented toys. Many pet shops sell hollow balls in which a treat or small amount of food can be hidden.

Catnip braid

Toys

Cats like toys that appeal to their chasing, stalking, and pouncing instincts. Suitable toys include small, lightweight balls and beanbags, felt or rope mice, pom-poms, and feathers. Items dangled from poles are ideal for grabbing or batting with the paws and running after. Make sure that toys are in good condition, with no pieces that could fall off and be swallowed. Most cats find wind-up or battery-operated toys that move around the floor particularly exciting.

Cheaper options

You don't need to buy your cat expensive accessories or toys. Cats can make their own amusement from simple, everyday items such as crumpled newspaper, cotton reels, pencils, pine cones, corks, and feathers. Cats love hiding, so provide yours with somewhere to play hide-and-seek, such as an old cardboard box or paper bag. Never let a cat play with a plastic bag – a cat can suffocate inside or strangle itself if it gets trapped in the handles.

PLAYSTATION
This multi-activity centre provides plenty of variety for your cat, with a cosy hiding place, scratching posts, somewhere to sit, and hanging balls to play with.

EXPLORING AND HIDING
Paper bags appeal to a cat's sense of curiosity, giving him something to investigate and hide in. Monitor your cat and make sure he can get out whenever he wants to.

New tricks

One way to make playtime with your cat more interesting is to teach him a new trick (p.233). Unlike a dog, which will learn tricks to please its "pack leader", a cat needs a different motivator – food. The best time to teach your cat is just before a meal, when he is hungry. Select a quiet spot with no distractions, but don't spend more than a few minutes on each training session. You may need to repeat the training a few times each day for several weeks, depending on your cat's age and the difficulty of the trick. Reward your cat's progress in getting the trick right with small treats, and make sure you give him plenty of praise. Your cat will only be willing to participate if he is having a good time: don't try to force him to do something he doesn't want to, and don't get cross if he decides he isn't interested.

GROOMING AND HYGIENE

Cats instinctively groom themselves, spending much of their time keeping their fur clean, tangle-free, and conditioned. However, many cats, especially longhaired breeds, show cats, and older cats, will need some assistance from their owners. Helping out with basic hygiene, such as teeth cleaning and bathing, is also essential to keep your cat in peak condition.

A cat spends many hours grooming itself

Natural grooming

Grooming keeps your cat's coat in prime condition. This is important because a sleek, conditioned coat is waterproof, keeps your cat warm, and protects his skin from infection. Grooming can also help keep your cat cool in hot weather.

Your cat will always groom himself in the same order. He begins by licking his lips and paws, then using his wet paws to clean the sides of his head. The saliva removes the scent of recent meals, making him "odourless" to natural enemies that hunt by scent. Next, your cat will use his rough tongue to groom his front legs, shoulders, and sides. The tongue is covered in tiny hooks that can get rid of mats and tangles in the coat. The tongue also spreads the natural oils secreted by glands in the skin that condition and waterproof the coat. Your cat will nibble away any stubborn tangles using his small incisors. His flexible spine then allows him to attend to his anal region, back legs, and tail, working from its base to the tip. He then uses his back paws like a wide-toothed comb to scratch his head. Cats raised together may sometimes groom each other, strengthening the bond between them.

Grooming your cat

Helping your cat maintain his coat is essential for several reasons. For a start, grooming sessions will enable you to maintain a close bond with your cat and also give you a chance to check his body for health problems. Some cats – especially those selectively bred for their long, soft hair, such as Persians – have difficulty keeping their coat clean and tangle-free on their own. When you groom your cat, you will help reduce the amount of hair he swallows while grooming himself. This hair is usually coughed up as fur balls. Some fur balls, however, pass through the stomach and get lodged in the intestine, causing serious problems. Cats become less efficient at grooming themselves as they get older, so elderly cats benefit greatly from a helping hand.

If you accustom your cat to grooming sessions from an early age, he will come to view you as a parent figure and enjoy the experience. Always begin a grooming session by stroking your cat and talking in a soothing voice to help him relax. Remember to be patient and on the look out for signs that he is uncomfortable, such as a flicking tail or whiskers turning forwards. In such cases, stop and try again later or the next day. Make sure you also check his ears, eyes, nose, and teeth, and clean them if necessary. You may also need to clip his claws, empty his scent-secreting anal sacs (or ask your vet to do this), and give him a bath. Always end a grooming session with praise and a treat.

GROOMING TOOLS

Basic utensils for cat grooming include combs (flea, fine, and wide toothed), brushes (slicker, pin tipped, or soft bristled), a rubber grooming glove, clippers, a cat toothbrush, and a tick remover. Some breeds may require specific tools for their coat type.

Tick remover

Nail clippers **Slicker brush** **Fine comb** **Soft-bristled brush**

GROOMING | SHORTHAIRED CAT

Shorthaired coats are easy to maintain, and most cats with such a coat cope well on their own, keeping their fur in tip-top condition. However, a once-a-week groom (twice weekly if you have a show cat) will help you maintain a close bond with your cat and allow you to check for any potential health issues, such as lumps or skin problems. Shorthaired cats generally benefit from a comb through with a flea or fine-toothed comb, then a brush to clear out loosened hair and dead skin, and finally a "polish" with a soft cloth, such as a chamois leather or piece of silk to produce an eye-catching sheen. Make sure you are careful when touching sensitive areas, such as the ears, armpits, belly, and tail. If your cat has rexed, or crimped, hair, use a very soft brush or a rubber grooming glove – anything harder may cause discomfort.

LOOSENING OLD HAIR AND DEAD SKIN
Draw a fine-toothed metal comb from head to tail, along the lie of the fur. This will loosen dead hair and skin cells. Be careful when grooming around the ears, the underside (armpits, belly, and groin), and the tail.

DEBRIS REMOVAL
Work over your cat's body with a slicker or soft-bristled brush, again along the lie of the fur. The brushing will get rid of all the debris loosened by the combing. Finish by polishing with a soft cloth.

GROOMING | LONGHAIRED CAT

Longhaired cats need much more grooming than shorthairs, ideally 15–30 minutes per day. Long fur, especially if it is soft and downy, picks up dirt and tangles easily, particularly in the armpit, groin, and anal regions, and behind the ears. These tangles prevent the coat from protecting the cat properly, making the skin vulnerable to damage and infection.

The main aim of grooming longhaired cats is to eliminate the tangles. Cat talcum powder can help tease them out, but with severely knotted tangles the only solution is to cut them out with scissors. Make sure the scissor tips point outwards, so that you do not cut the skin. If you are unsure about this, take your cat to a professional groomer or ask your vet to do it.

INITIAL COMBING
Comb the fur against the lie from the roots outwards. Unscented talc will help tease out tangles and also remove excess oils. Work through again with a finer comb. Take care combing the tail and underside.

BRUSHING OUT LOOSENED DEBRIS
Brush out loose debris and any remaining talc with a soft-bristled or pin-tipped brush. Work against the lie. Fluff out the coat with the brush or a wide-toothed comb. With a Persian, comb neck fur up into a ruff.

How to bathe your cat

Outdoor cats occasionally give themselves a dust bath, in which they roll in dry earth to clean their coat of grease and parasites, such as fleas. You can buy dry shampoos for cats, which work in a similar way. A shorthaired cat may need a wet bath if it becomes covered in oil or a pungent substance. A longhaired cat requires more frequent bathing. Few cats enjoy being bathed, and it's easier for both of you if you accustom your cat to the experience from an early age.

When bathing your cat, you will need to be patient. Use soothing words throughout the session and give treats to your cat afterwards as a reward. Before you begin, close all doors and windows, and make sure the room is warm and free of draughts. Prior to bathing your cat, brush his coat thoroughly. You can wash your cat in a bathtub or a sink using a shower attachment, but make sure the water flow is quite weak. Line the bottom of the bath or sink with a rubber mat for your cat to grip, so he feels secure and will not slip.

GROOMING | BATHING A CAT

1 Lower your cat into a bathtub or place him in a sink, talking to him soothingly. Spray him with warm water that is as near to body temperature (38.6°C/101.5°F) as possible. Soak his fur thoroughly.

2 Always apply a special cat shampoo. Never use dog shampoo, as it might contain a flea-killing chemical that is toxic to cats. Avoid getting shampoo in your cat's eyes, ears, nose, or mouth.

3 Lather in the shampoo thoroughly, then rinse it off completely. Repeat the shampoo wash or rub in a conditioner and rinse off again. Remember to keep giving your cat plenty of praise.

4 Towel-dry your cat, or use an electric dryer on a low setting if the noise doesn't upset him. Brush his coat and allow him to finish drying off in a warm room. Give your cat a well-earned treat.

Cleaning ears, eyes, and nose

The inside of your cat's ears should be clean and free of odour. Remove excess earwax with cotton wool or tissue. If you see dark, gritty specks in the ears, which indicate ear mites, or an ear discharge, take your cat to the vet. Damp cotton wool can also be used to clean around the eyes and nose. Mucus may collect in the corners of the eyes of long-muzzled cats, such as Siamese. Short-faced cats, such as Persians, often suffer from tear overflow, which leaves mahogany stains on the fur around the eyes. Consult your vet if you find any discharge from the eyes or nose, or prolonged redness of the eyes.

REMOVING EAR WAX
Use cotton wool or tissue, dampened with either water or an ear-cleaning solution from your vet. Never use cotton buds, because you might push wax further into the ear canal.

TEETH CLEANING

- **Hold the head** firmly, prise open the jaws, and clean each tooth for a few seconds.

- **Use a child's** toothbrush or a specially made cat's toothbrush, some of which fit on to a finger.

- **Special cat toothpastes** are available. Your cat will especially enjoy the meat-flavoured ones.

- **If your cat** won't allow you to brush his teeth, ask your vet for oral antiseptics, which you apply directly to the cat's gums.

GROOMING | NAIL CLIPPING

How to clip your cat's nails

Cats naturally keep their nails worn down by exercise, scratching, climbing, and biting. Indoor and especially older cats often don't get much claw-wearing exercise and are at risk of growing long claws that curl into the pads of the paws, causing discomfort. To prevent this, regularly check your cat's claws and cut them with clippers about every two weeks. Keep a firm hold on your cat and make sure you remove just the very end of the claw. Any further down and you might cut into the pink region, or "quick", and cause pain and bleeding. If you find it too difficult, ask your vet to cut your cat's nails instead.

EXTENDING THE CLAW
When clipping your cat's claws, very gently press down on the bone just behind each claw with your fingers to make the claw extend fully.

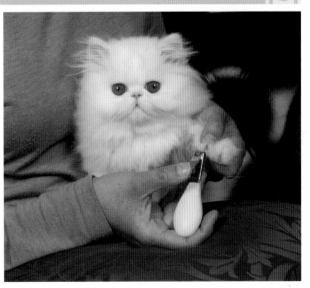

START THEM YOUNG
Accustom your cat to having his nails clipped from an early age. If your cat is not in the mood and struggles, don't force things. Let him go, and try again the next day.

TRAINING YOUR CAT

Training your cat may sound a strange, if not impossible, thing to do and contrary to the nature of such a free-spirited animal. But basic training, such as teaching your cat to sit, has benefits, and some cats make willing pupils. Training your cat will make it easier for you to control and manage his behaviour. You may even be able to teach him a few tricks or train him to walk on a harness and lead.

Cat with harness

Anything for food

Cats are happy to learn if there's an edible reward. Unlike dogs, cats don't respond to discipline. Simply calling to your cat will not teach him to sit or come to you, but a tasty titbit – such as a dried chicken treat or a dehydrated prawn – and lots of gentle praise will help greatly. Cats learn best when hungry; just before meals is ideal. During training, break treats into small portions. Too many too soon and your cat will stop feeling hungry and lose interest. Cats learn best from about four months old. Young kittens lack concentration; old cats are generally not interested. Active shorthaired cats, such as Siamese, are generally easier to train than other breeds.

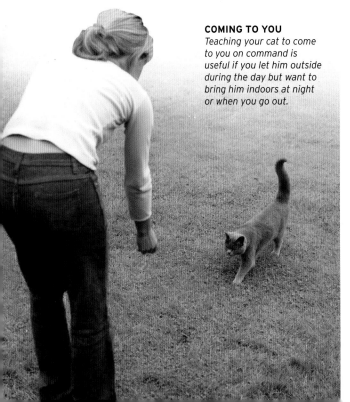

COMING TO YOU
Teaching your cat to come to you on command is useful if you let him outside during the day but want to bring him indoors at night or when you go out.

Basic training

Your cat cannot be trained unless he has a name – preferably a short name of one or two syllables that he will find easy to recognize and respond to. If you've adopted an adult cat, it's best not to change his name, even if you dislike it. Training sessions should last for one or two minutes, never much longer, and preferably in a quiet room, free of distractions.

To get a cat to come to you, call him by his name while tempting him with a treat. As he approaches, take a step back and say "Come". When he has walked up to you, give the treat and praise him. Repeat this, increasing the distance each time until he will run to you from another room on hearing your command. If you then phase out the treats, he should still respond to your call.

Miaow on cue

Once your cat has learned to come when called, you can try training him to miaow on cue. Hold a treat in your hand and call to him, but withhold the treat until he miaows – even if he tries to swipe the morsel from your hand. As soon as he does miaow, say his name and at the same time hand over the treat. Practise both with and without giving a treat to reinforce the behaviour, until your cat always miaows at the sound of his name. You can then begin to phase out the treats.

ATTRACTING ATTENTION
When your cat can miaow in response to his name, it will help you to find him. It could even be a life-saving skill if he becomes trapped somewhere.

LEARNING TO SIT
When your cat has learned to come when you call his name, you can then start to teach him to sit. If he can sit without fidgeting, it will be much easier to groom him or have him examined by a vet.

The sit command

To teach a cat to sit, place him on a table so that he is standing on all fours. Gain his attention with a treat and hold it a few centimetres above his head. If the treat is too far away he will be inclined to rise up on his hindlegs and bat it from your hand. Slowly move the treat over your cat's head and between his ears, and as he watches it he will sit back. Say his name, then say "Sit" as he begins to sit. Once he is sitting, say "Good sit" and give the treat. After about ten sessions, simply holding your hand over his head should be enough to make him sit.

Walking an indoor cat outside

You can give your indoor cat a taste of the outside world by walking him on a lead. Cats need a harness rather than just a collar, which they can easily slip their head out of. First, allow your cat to get used to wearing the harness. Put it on him for 20 minutes each day for a few days. Give treats and praise, and make sure it fits correctly. Next, clip on the lead and let him stroll around indoors with it dangling, again for short periods, and then with you holding the lead. Finally, venture outside, ideally somewhere quiet. Your cat will initially spend most of his time sniffing and looking around and leading you. Never pull the lead in the direction you want to go; instead, persuade him with gentle commands and treats. Within a few weeks, he will be relaxed when walking with you outdoors.

Fun tricks

Once your cat has learned to come to you and to sit on command, you can go on to teach him some tricks, such as sitting up on his hindlegs, waving his paw, exchanging a high five, retrieving thrown cat toys, or even jumping through a hoop. To get your cat to sit up, or beg, for example, hold a treat above his head and when he rises give the treat to him and say "Good up". To get your sitting cat to high five you, hold a teaser toy, such as feathers on the end of a stick, in front of him. As he raises his paw to the toy, say "Good high five" or "All right!" and give him a reward. After several lessons, use your hand rather than the toy. Then gradually phase out the treats until you are just using clear hand signals and verbal cues.

The same principles apply for teaching tricks as they do for basic training: hold one- to two-minute sessions before meals, when your cat is hungry and willing to earn his food. Always remember to be patient and to give plenty of gentle praise. Don't try to persevere if your cat is not in the right mood.

THE WAVE
Cats can also master fun tricks, such as waving a paw, if you make the experience an enjoyable and rewarding one for them.

BEHAVIOUR PROBLEMS

Pet cats sometimes have (what we humans consider) behaviour problems, such as sudden aggression, scratching furniture, spraying urine, and refusing to use the litter tray. Such actions make perfect sense - to a cat. Your job is to try to find out whether the behaviour is down to illness or stress, or just a case of a cat following his instincts. You will then, with patience, be able to solve or minimize the problem.

A stressed cat may be very destructive

Aggression

If your cat bites or scratches when you're playing with him, stop play immediately. He is probably becoming overexcited or does not want you touching a sensitive area, such as his belly. Don't use your hands as "toys" when playing with him, as it will encourage him to bite or scratch them. Rough play may trigger aggression, so make sure your children play gently and know when to leave him alone. Any pet dogs must be trained not to tease your cat, to avoid a backlash. If your cat likes to ambush ankles or jump on shoulders, anticipate this and throw your cat a toy to play with instead.

Should your cat become aggressive for no obvious reason, he may be lashing out because he is in pain, so take him to the vet. Long-term aggression may result from your cat not having been socialized properly as a kitten. He may always remain wary of humans, but be patient and you may eventually gain his trust. In general, cats are much more docile after neutering.

Chewing and scratching

Boredom may lead to stress and destructive behaviour. A cat that spends his life indoors, especially if he is often alone, may chew household objects to relieve the tedium. If this sounds like your cat, give him plenty of toys to play with, and make sure you set aside some special time each day when you give him your full attention. Scratching is natural cat behaviour that sharpens the claws and makes a visible and scented sign of a cat's territory. If your sofa is becoming heavily scratched, buy a scratching post as an alternative for your cat to mark his territory. If he prefers to claw at the carpet, provide a horizontal scratching mat instead. Make sure that the material covering the post is different from that

CATS AT WAR

Aggression may occur between two previously friendly cats after an upset in their routines. For example, a cat that has spent some time away from home, such as at the vet, may be greeted with hostility on his return.

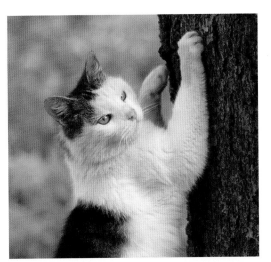

TERRITORIAL SIGN
Scratching tree bark is natural feline behaviour. It leaves a visible and scented sign to other cats, warning them that they are now trespassing on another cat's patch.

SCRATCHING POST
Your cat will continue his territorial behaviour indoors (see left), so give him a dedicated scratching post to minimize damage to furniture.

of the sofa. Place the post close to where your cat has been scratching. Rub some catnip into the post to tempt him if he is reluctant to use it. If he persists in scratching the furniture, deter him further by cleaning the scratched area to take away his scent – use surgical spirit, because cats hate the smell. Then cover the area in something that cats dislike the feel of, such as double-sided sticky tape.

If he still will not stop, gently spray your cat's rump (never his head) with a water pistol whenever he scratches. You can also minimize damage from scratching by gluing small, plastic caps over your cat's claws. These are available from pet shops, but should only be used for permanently indoor cats.

Spraying

Like scratching, spraying marks territory too, but this behaviour usually disappears once a cat is neutered. It may recur if your cat becomes stressed by a change in his environment, such as the arrival of a baby or another pet.

To combat indoor spraying, distract your cat the moment you see him raise his tail to spray. Push his tail down or throw him a toy. If there is an area he sprays repeatedly, cleanse it thoroughly and place his food bowls there to deter further spraying. You can also line sprayed areas with aluminium foil, because cats dislike the sound of their urine hitting it.

Litter-tray problems

If your cat experiences pain when relieving himself, he may associate his discomfort with the litter tray and go elsewhere. So when he relieves himself outside the tray, seek a vet's advice. An all-clear from the vet will mean that the problem is probably down to something you are doing. If waste is not removed from the tray frequently, your cat may find the tray's odour overpowering. Similarly, adding a cover to the tray, to shield the smell from you, may make the smell inside too much for him. Switching to a new type of litter can also cause problems, since your cat may find its texture unpleasant (p.211).

TOP TIPS

■ **To stop your cat nibbling** houseplants, coat the leaves in a strong-scented citrus spray that cats dislike.

■ **A pheromone treatment** from a vet can solve aggression or anxiety-related spraying.

■ **If you have two** indoor cats, give each a litter tray. Some cats don't like sharing.

HEALTH AND BREEDING

HEALTH

Your greatest responsibility as an owner is your cat's health. You must ensure that your pet has regular check-ups and vaccinations, and be able to recognize any changes in his body or behaviour that may require a trip to the vet. Educate yourself about common disorders and learn how to care for your cat when he is ill, recovering from surgery, or in an emergency.

Keep your cat free of itchy parasites

Finding and visiting a vet

Before bringing a cat home, look for a veterinary practice at which to register your cat. Your cat breeder may be able to recommend one. Alternatively, ask friends with cats or consult a local cat club or rescue centre. Going to the vet is stressful for most cats, because they encounter strangers and other animals. Even a well-socialized cat will feel uneasy during the visit. Always take your cat in a carrier, with its door kept facing you in the waiting room so that he can see you. Speak to him soothingly and reward him with treats afterwards.

If you buy a pedigree kitten, he should already have had his first vaccinations before you take him home at about 12 weeks old. Your breeder will give you the kitten's vaccination certificate, which you should show the vet on your initial visit. One of your earliest visits may be to have your cat neutered, generally from four months of age.

EAR EXAMINATION
Your vet will examine the ears for mites during a routine check-up. Ear mites are highly contagious and commonly affect kittens and outdoor cats. They leave gritty debris in the ear canal that causes skin irritation.

Annual check-ups

After his first visits, your cat will need a check-up annually, possibly twice a year in his old age. The vet will assess his condition by checking his ears, eyes, teeth, gums, heartbeat, breathing, and weight, and feel him all over for abnormalities. A booster vaccination may be given. Your vet may clip your cat's claws if necessary, especially if he is a housecat or elderly. The vet will also inspect your cat for parasites and give you advice on administering worming and flea treatments.

INITIAL VACCINATION
Cats should have their first vaccinations against infectious diseases, such as cat flu and feline leukaemia, at between 9 and 12 weeks of age, followed by annual boosters for the rest of their lives.

THOROUGH EXAMINATION
During an annual check-up, the vet will examine your cat from head to tail, feeling for any tenderness or lumps. The vet will also listen to his heart and breathing, to ensure there are no irregularities.

Common health problems

Every cat will experience health problems during his lifetime. Some complaints, such as a one-off incident of vomiting or diarrhoea, are not a major cause for concern and do not require treatment by a vet. Other problems, such as intestinal worms or fleas, can be treated easily enough at home, following instructions from your vet. More serious disorders requiring urgent veterinary attention include: repeated vomiting or diarrhoea – often a sign of an underlying disorder; urinary tract infections or obstructions, which can cause painful urination; eye problems, such as conjunctivitis or a visible third eyelid; abscesses from fights with other cats; and painful dental problems preventing your cat from eating.

CAT OFF HIS FOOD
Refusing food is a cause for concern. It may indicate that your cat is in pain or has a serious illness needing urgent veterinary attention.

Signs of poor health

Cats tend to suffer in silence and do not draw attention to themselves when they are feeling vulnerable. One of your responsibilities as an owner is to be vigilant, keeping an eye out for any changes in your cat's routines and behaviour that might suggest he needs veterinary attention.

Lethargy is difficult to spot – because cats generally rest much of the time – but decreased levels of activity, a reluctance to jump, and reduced alertness are often signs that your cat is ill or in pain. Lethargy is also often linked to obesity, so it may disappear when a cat loses his excess weight.

Changes in appetite are usually a sign of an underlying condition. A loss of appetite may be caused by pain in the mouth, such as toothache, or a more serious illness, such as kidney failure. Weight loss despite an increased appetite, together with increased urination and increased thirst, may be the result of an overactive thyroid or diabetes mellitus.

Abnormal or laboured breathing may occur after a chest injury or as a result of an obstruction in the airway, an upper respiratory tract infection, or shock. Wheezing may be due to asthma or bronchitis. Breathing difficulties always require an emergency trip to the vet.

Dehydration is life-threatening and has various causes, including vomiting, diarrhoea, increased urination, and heatstroke. You can carry out a simple test to check if your cat is dehydrated (see box left). Emergency rehydration involves a vet injecting fluids under the skin or directly into a vein.

The colour of a cat's gums (see box left) can indicate several serious disorders, including those that affect the circulation of oxygen in the bloodstream. Lumps on skin, changes in grooming habits and coat texture, fur loss, and not using the litter tray can also be signs of health problems.

TOP TIPS

■ **Dehydration test** Gently lift the skin up on the back of your cat's neck. If the skin springs back into position, your cat is healthy, but if it returns slowly it is a sign of dehydration. Feel the gums with a finger – dry, tacky gums also indicate dehydration.

■ **Checking gums** A healthy cat has pink gums. Pale or white gums indicate shock, anaemia, or blood loss; yellow gums are a sign of jaundice; red gums are caused by carbon-monoxide poisoning, fever, or bleeding in the mouth; blue gums suggest poor oxygenation of the blood.

First aid for cats

If your cat is injured, you may need to administer first aid before he has a chance to be seen by a vet. To treat a wound, apply pressure with a pad of clean cloth or gauze. Do not use tissue because it will stick to the wound. Keep the material in place, even if it becomes soaked with blood, until you see a vet. Removing an object embedded in a wound could cause more bleeding – leave it in place for your vet to treat.

A cat that has had an accident, such as being hit by a car, should be seen by a vet even if he has no visible injuries, as there could be internal bleeding, which can lead to shock.

TREATING SHOCK
A cat in shock may suffer from heat loss. Wrap him loosely in a blanket or fleece until he is assessed by a vet.

Shock is a life-threatening condition in which there is reduced blood flow, and tissues become starved of nutrients. Symptoms of shock include irregular breathing, anxiety, pale or blue gums, and a lowered body temperature. First aid for a cat in shock involves keeping him warm and elevating his hindquarters to increase blood flow to the brain while you take him to a vet.

If you find your cat unconscious, make sure his airway is not obstructed, listen and look for breathing, and feel for a pulse with a finger on one of the femoral arteries, which can be found on the inner side of his hindlegs, where they meet the groin. If there is no breathing, attempt artificial respiration by gently blowing air into your cat's lungs down the nostrils. If there is no heartbeat, alternate two breaths of artificial respiration with thirty chest compressions at two compressions per second.

ELIZABETHAN COLLAR
After surgery your cat may have to wear an Elizabethan collar for several days to prevent him from licking or chewing a wound that may have been stitched to help it repair.

BANDAGED LEG
A leg wound requires bandaging by a vet. Keep your cat inside if he has a bandaged limb. If the dressing becomes dirty, wet, loose, smelly, or uncomfortable, take your cat back to the vet for it to be changed.

When your cat is unwell

If your cat is ill or recovering from surgery or an accident, you must resist the temptation to stroke and cuddle him. He will most likely not enjoy being handled in the early stages of convalescence. Stroke or pet your cat only if he clearly wants attention. Provide him with a warm bed, where he can be left in peace to recuperate. Check on your cat regularly and change the bedding if it becomes soiled. If you have an outdoor cat, make sure he is kept indoors during his recovery and has easy access to bowls of water and a litter tray.

Administering medicine

Only give your cat medicine prescribed by a vet, and follow the instructions carefully. You can try hiding a pill in a ball of meat or mould a sticky treat around it, but only if your cat is allowed to take food with his medicine. If not, or if he rejects or coughs up the pill, you will need to place it in his mouth (see below). This is best done with a helper to hold your cat while you insert the pill. If you are on your own, immobilize your cat by wrapping him in a towel, leaving his head exposed. Liquid medicines are also widely available and should be instilled into the mouth, between the back teeth and cheek, using a plastic syringe without a needle or a plastic medicine dropper. Drops for the eyes or ears can be administered while gently immobilizing your cat's head. Always make sure that the dropper does not touch his eyes or ears.

If your cat is wholly resistant to being given any kind of medicine at home, take him to your vet each day or have him kept at the practice until the course of treatment is over.

TOP TIPS

Caring for a convalescing cat:

■ Give frequent small portions of food heated to body temperature. You may have to hand-feed him initially.

■ Check your cat's wounds daily for redness or infection.

■ Provide a cosy bed, in a quiet location, with a microwavable heating pad or a hot-water bottle wrapped in a towel.

■ Keep other pets away from your cat while he is recuperating.

■ Give medicine according to your vet's instructions.

HEALTH | GIVING A PILL

1 Hold your cat's head with forefinger and thumb on either side of his mouth. Gently tilt his head back and pry open his jaws.

2 Place the pill as far back as possible on his tongue to trigger swallowing. Give him gentle encouragement while doing so.

Massaging your cat's throat for several seconds will make him swallow the pill

3 Close your cat's mouth and gently massage his throat to make sure the pill has been swallowed properly. Reward with praise and give him a treat.

OVERWEIGHT CAT
If you cannot easily feel your cat's ribs or see a waist towards the back of his abdomen, he is overweight.

Weight problems

Various health problems are associated with obesity, including diabetes, cardiovascular disease, liver disease, and arthritis and mobility problems resulting from strain on joints. Weight gain may also make it difficult for your cat to groom himself.

If your cat is noticeably gaining weight, switch him to a low-calorie diet, provide fewer treats and meals, and increase his levels of exercise. Neutered cats are particularly at risk of weight gain, as are indoor cats, which may not exercise enough. Outdoor cats can put on weight if other people feed them too. Cats usually live longer if they are a healthy weight.

Weight loss is also a cause for concern and should always be checked by a vet. It may be a sign of a serious disorder, such as an overactive thyroid gland.

Caring for an older cat

Most well-cared-for pet cats can live to age 14 or 15, with some occasionally reaching 20. The trend for cat life expectancy is upwards, with advances in disease prevention, a better understanding of diet, improved drugs and treatments, and more cats being kept indoors.

By about age ten, you may notice signs of ageing in your cat: weight loss (or gain), deteriorating eyesight, dental disease, a decrease in mobility, less fastidious grooming, and a thinner, less shiny coat. His personality may change too, with your cat becoming easily irritated and noisier, especially at night. As a senior, he may occasionally feel disorientated and relieve himself outside the litter tray. You may want to start increasing his regular check-ups by a vet to twice a year.

COMPARING LIFESPANS

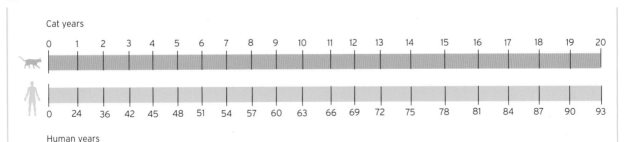

Cat years

| 0 | 1 | 2 | 3 | 4 | 5 | 6 | 7 | 8 | 9 | 10 | 11 | 12 | 13 | 14 | 15 | 16 | 17 | 18 | 19 | 20 |

| 0 | 24 | 36 | 42 | 45 | 48 | 51 | 54 | 57 | 60 | 63 | 66 | 69 | 72 | 75 | 78 | 81 | 84 | 87 | 90 | 93 |

Human years

It is often said that one year of a cat's life equates to seven years of a human's. But this does not hold, as life expectancy for pet cats has risen in recent years. It also ignores the different rates at which cats and humans develop: a one-year-old cat can breed and raise kittens, which is a far more advanced stage than that of a seven-year-old child. By about three, a cat is roughly equivalent to a person in their early 40s. Each cat year from then on corresponds to about three human years. Use the chart above to find an approximate "human age" for your cat.

INHERITED DISORDERS

Some diseases and disorders are passed down from one generation of cats to the next. Different cat breeds have their own inherited health problems, usually as a result of inbreeding among a relatively small population. Responsible breeders should not breed from cats known to have faulty genes, and screening tests for many of these disorders are now available.

Cats with flat faces may suffer from breathing difficulties

Breed-specific problems

Because the gene pool may be quite small for each cat breed, faulty genes can have a greater influence than they would in a larger mixed-cat population, where such genes usually vanish after a few generations. Some cat breeds are even characterized by inherited disorders – for example, in the past the crossed eyes of classic Siamese cats were the result of a visual problem. An inherited disorder may be present when a kitten is born or develop later in a cat's life. Some cats may have a faulty gene but never develop any symptoms. These cats are called carriers, and can produce kittens with the inherited disease if they breed with another cat carrying the same faulty gene.

Many cat diseases are thought to be genetic in origin, but have not yet had faulty genes identified to explain them. The disorders in the table below have all been confirmed as genetic. For some of them, screening tests are available to identify whether or not a cat has the faulty gene. To help eradicate inherited disorders, responsible breeders should avoid using any cats known to have or to carry an inherited disorder for breeding by having them neutered.

If your cat has, or develops, an inherited disorder, try to find out as much information as possible about the condition. Most inherited disorders are not curable, but careful management can reduce symptoms and allow a good quality of life for your pet.

DISEASE	DESCRIPTION	CAN IT BE SCREENED FOR?	MANAGING THE DISEASE	BREEDS OF CAT AFFECTED
Primary seborrhoea	Flaky or greasy skin and hair.	No specific screening test available.	Wash the affected cat frequently with medicated shampoo.	Persian, Exotic
Congenital hypotrichosis	Kittens are born with no hair and are susceptible to infection.	No test currently available for this rare disorder.	No treatment. Keep the cat in a warm indoor environment, away from potential sources of infection.	Birman
Bleeding disorders	Excessive or abnormal bleeding after injury or trauma.	Yes. There are tests available for some types of bleeding disorder.	Look for non-healing wounds on your cat. Try to staunch blood flow and seek veterinary advice.	Birman, British Shorthair, Devon Rex
Pyruvate kinase deficiency	A condition that affects life span and the number of red blood cells, leading to anaemia.	Yes. A genetic test is available.	Affected cats may need blood transfusions.	Abyssinian, Somali

DISEASE	DESCRIPTION	CAN IT BE SCREENED FOR?	MANAGING THE DISEASE	BREEDS OF CAT AFFECTED
Glycogenosis	Inability to metabolize glucose properly, leading to severe muscle weakness then heart failure.	Yes. A genetic test is available.	No treatment. Affected cats will need short-term fluid therapy.	Norwegian Forest Cat
Hypertrophic cardiomyopathy	Thickening of the heart muscle, usually results in heart failure.	Yes. A genetic test is available.	Drugs may be given to minimize the effects of heart failure.	Maine Coon, Ragdoll
Spinal muscular atrophy	Progressive muscular weakness, beginning in the hind limbs. Appears in kittens from 15 weeks old.	Yes. A genetic test is available.	No treatment. In some cases, an affected cat may survive with an adequate quality of life if given support.	Maine Coon
Devon Rex myopathy	General muscle weakness, an abnormal gait, and problems with swallowing.	No. Disorder first appears in kittens at 3–4 weeks old.	No treatment. Give affected cats small, liquid meals to avoid risk of choking.	Devon Rex
Hypokalaemic polymyopathy	Muscle weakness, associated with kidney failure. Affected cats often have a stiff gait and head tremors.	Yes. A genetic test is available for Burmese cats.	The condition can be managed with oral potassium.	Burmese, Asians
Lysosomal storage disease	Any of various enzyme deficiencies that affect many body systems, including the nervous system.	Yes. Some types of the disease can be screened and tested for.	No effective treatment. Affected cats usually die young.	Persian, Exotic, Siamese, Oriental, Balinese, Burmese, Asians, Korat
Polycystic kidney disease	Pockets of fluid (cysts) develop in the kidneys, eventually causing kidney failure.	Yes. A genetic test is available.	No cure. Drugs can be given to ease the workload of the kidneys.	British Shorthair, Persian, Exotic
Progressive retinal atrophy	Degeneration of the rods and cones in the retina of the eyes, leading to early blindness.	Yes. There is a test available for one form of the disorder, found in Abyssinians and Somalis.	No cure. Affected cats should be kept as safe as possible, away from potential hazards.	Abyssinian, Somali, Persian, Exotic
Osteochondrodysplasia	Painful degenerative joint disorder, leading to the fusion of tail, ankle, and knee bones.	No. To help prevent the disorder, cats with folded ears should only be crossed with cats with normal ears.	Palliative treatment can help ease pain and swelling of joints.	Scottish Fold
Manx syndrome	A condition where the spine is too short, leading to spinal-cord damage and affecting the bladder, bowels, and digestion.	No. There is no specific test for this severe form of taillessness.	No treatment. Most kittens are euthanized when the disease becomes apparent.	Manx

SPONSIBLE BREEDING

Breeding pedigree cats may sound like an enjoyable - and potentially lucrative - endeavour, but becoming a breeder is a big commitment. Most successful breeders have years of experience behind them. If you decide to go ahead, be ready to put lots of time (and money) into research, preparation, and caring for your pregnant cat and her newborn kittens.

A litter often includes a mixture of coat colours

A big decision

Before trying your hand as a breeder, make sure you know what you are letting yourself in for. Get as much advice and detailed information as possible. The breeder from whom you bought your pedigree female cat will be able to give you valuable tips, including where to find a suitable pedigree tom to father the kittens. You will need a thorough understanding of cat genetics, especially coat colours and patterns, because the litter may have a mix of characteristics. You must also be aware of genetic diseases associated with your breed (pp.244-5). Pedigree kittens sell for hundreds of pounds, but most of this income will be offset by costs for the stud, veterinary fees, heating for the kittens, registration fees, and extra food for the mother and kittens (once they are weaned). There may also be the long-term cost of owning more cats if you can't find suitable homes for your kittens.

PREGNANT CAT
A domestic cat's pregnancy usually lasts for between 63 and 68 days.

Pregnancy and birth

If the mating was successful, your cat will be visibly pregnant by about four weeks. Give her extra food and ask your vet about any supplements she might need. Towards the end of her pregnancy, make a nest for her out of a cardboard box containing plain paper that she can tear up. You will need to be around for the birth to ensure it runs smoothly. Make sure you know what to expect - your vet can advise you about what will happen at each stage of the birth. After that, your main job will be to socialize the kittens so they'll be ready for new homes when they are about 12 weeks old.

HAND FEEDING
If a kitten is not thriving, you will need to feed him a cat-milk substitute from a pipette, about every two hours. Ask your vet about how to do this.

NEUTERING

Surgical sterilization, or neutering, is advised for any cat you don't intend to breed from. In males, the testes are removed in a simple operation. Neutered males rarely spray indoors. They are less aggressive and less likely to get injured in territorial battles or catch diseases from fighting or mating. Neutering females, called spaying, is major surgery in which the ovaries and part of the uterus are removed. It has a positive effect on longevity, eliminating the risk of common cancers in female cats.

HAPPY FAMILY
If all the kittens are healthy, the only assistance the mother will need will be extra food to help her produce milk for her litter. If she trusts you, she may let you handle her kittens from the start.

GLOSSARY

Albinism - Lack of the pigment that gives colour to skin, hair, and eyes. In cats true albinism is very rare, but partial albinism gives rise to pointed coat patterns, as in the Siamese, and colour variations such as silver tabby.

Almond-shaped eyes - Oval eyes with flattened corners, seen in breeds such as the Abyssinian and Siamese.

Awn hairs - Slightly longer bristly hairs that, together with the soft down hairs, constitute the undercoat.

Bicolour - Coat pattern combining white with another colour.

Blotched tabby - Alternative term for Classic Tabby.

Blue - Light to medium-grey coat colour, a dilute form of black. Blue-only cat breeds include the Russian Blue, Korat, and Chartreux.

Bracelets - Dark horizontal bands on the legs of a tabby cat.

Break - *see* Stop

Breeches - In longhaired cats, extra-long hair on the upper back part of the hindlegs.

Breed standard - Detailed description produced by a cat registry that defines the required standards for a pedigree cat's conformation, coat, and colour.

Calico - Name used in the USA for tortie and white patterning.

Cameo - Red, or its dilute form cream, where white covers two-thirds of the hair shaft.

Carnivore - Meat-eating animal.

Cat fancier - Enthusiast for breeding and showing pedigree cats.

Cat registry - Organization that sets breed standards and registers the pedigrees of cats.

CFA - The Cat Fanciers' Association, the world's largest registry of pedigree cats, based in North America.

Chocolate - Pale to medium-brown coat colour.

Chromosome - Thread-like structure within a cell nucleus, containing genes arranged along a strand of DNA. Cats have 38 chromosomes arranged in 19 corresponding pairs (humans have 46, arranged in 23 pairs).

Classic tabby - *see* Tabby

Cobby - Compact, muscular, heavy-boned body type, seen in breeds such as the Persian.

Colourpoint - *see* Pointed

Crossbreed - *see* Random-bred

Curled ears - Ears that curve backwards, as in the American Curl.

Dilute/dilution - Paler version of a colour caused by the dilution gene, for example when black becomes blue and red becomes cream.

Domestic cat - Any member of *Felis catus*, pedigree or mixed breed. Also commonly known as a housecat.

Dominant - Describes a gene inherited from one parent that overrides the effect of a paired recessive gene inherited from the other parent. For example, the gene for a tabby coat is dominant.

Down - Short, soft, fine hairs that form an undercoat in some breeds.

Double coat - Fur consisting of a thick, soft undercoat covered by a protective topcoat of longer guard hairs.

Feathering - Longer hair on areas such as legs, feet, and tail.

Feral - Describing a domesticated species that has reverted to a wild state.

FIFe - Fédération Internationale Féline, the leading European federation of cat registries.

Folded ears - Ears that fold forwards and downwards, seen in breeds such as the Scottish Fold.

GCCF - The Governing Council of the Cat Fancy, the leading organization for the registration of cats in the UK.

Gene pool - The complete collection of genes within an interbreeding population.

Ghost markings - Faint tabby markings on the coat of a self-coloured cat that show up in certain lights.

Ground colour - Background colour in tabbies; there are many variants: brown, red, and silver are among the most common.

Guard hairs - Longer, tapering hairs that form a cat's topcoat and provide weatherproofing.

Hybrid - Offspring of two different species - for example the Bengal, which is a cross between the domestic cat (*Felis catus*) and the Asian leopard cat (*Felis bengalensis*).

Leather - Hairless area at the end of the nose. Colour varies according to coat colour and is defined in the breed standards for pedigree cats.

Lilac - Warm pink-grey colour, a dilute form of brown.

Mackerel tabby - *see* Tabby

"M" mark - Typical "M"-shaped mark on the forehead of tabby cats; also known as a "frown" mark.

Marbled - Variation of the Classic Tabby, mostly seen in wildcat hybrids such as the Bengal.

Mascara lines - Dark lines running from the outer corners of the eyes, or encircling the eyes.

Mask - Dark coloration on the face, usually around the muzzle and eyes.

"Moggie" - Informal term for a non-pedigree cat.

Mitted - Colour pattern in which the paws are white. Also called mittens or socks.

Mutation - Change in a cell's DNA, often arising by chance; effects of genetic mutations in cats include hairlessness, folded or curled ears, curly coats, and short tails.

Parti-colour - General term for a coat pattern that has two or more colours; often one being white.

Pedigree - Pure-bred.

Pointed - Coat pattern in which a cat has pale body fur with darker extremities (head, tail, and legs); typically seen in the Siamese.

Polydactyly - Extra toes produced by a genetic mutation; polydactyly, or polydactylism, is common in certain breeds, but only in the Pixiebob is the trait accepted in the breed standard.

Random-bred - Cat of mixed parentage.

Recessive - A gene that can produce an effect only when inherited from both parents. If a recessive gene from one parent is paired with a dominant gene from the other parent, its effect will be overridden. The genes for certain eye colours and long fur in cats are recessive.

Rex coat - Curly or wavy coat, as seen in Devon and Cornish Rex cats.

Ruff - Frill of longer hair around the neck and chest.

Selective breeding - Mating of animals that possess desired traits, such as a particular coat colour or pattern.

Self - Coat in which a single colour is distributed evenly along the hair shaft; known as "solid" in the USA.

Semi-longhair - Medium-long coat, usually with a minimal undercoat.

Sepia - Dark-brown ticking on a paler ground colour.

Shaded - Coat pattern in which the final quarter of each hair is coloured.

Single coat - Coat with just one layer, usually the topcoat of guard hairs, seen in such cats as the Balinese and Turkish Angora.

Smoke - Coat pattern in which each hair shaft is pale at the base and coloured for about half of its length.

Sorrel - Reddish-brown, used to describe certain coat colours in Abyssinian and Somali cats; known as red in the USA.

Spotted tabby - *see* Tabby

Stop - Indentation between the muzzle and the top of the head; also known as a break.

Tabby - Genetically dominant coat pattern that comes in four types: Classic Tabby has a blotched or whorled pattern; Mackerel Tabby has "fishbone" stripes; Spotted Tabby has spots or rosettes; Ticked Tabbies have a faint pattern on a ticked coat.

Temperament - The character of a cat.

TICA - The International Cat Association, a genetic registry for pedigree cats worldwide.

Ticked - Coat pattern in which each hair shaft has alternate bands of pale and darker colours; also known as agouti. See also Tabby.

Tipped - Coat pattern in which just the tip of each hair is strongly coloured.

Topcoat - Outer coat of guard hairs.

Tortie - Common abbreviation for tortoiseshell.

Tortie and white - Tortoiseshell with a high proportion of white fur; known as calico in the USA.

Tortie-tabby - Tortoiseshell with tabby markings; known as "patched tabby" in the USA.

Tortoiseshell - Coat pattern in which black and red hairs, or their dilute forms, are mixed in patches.

Tricolour - Term sometimes used to describe a coat of two colours plus white.

Tufts - Clusters of longer hairs, which are seen, for example, between the toes or on the ears.

Undercoat - Layer of hair beneath the topcoat, usually short and often woolly.

Usual - A colour of Abyssinian cats - known as "ruddy" in the USA.

Van pattern - Pointed coat pattern in which the colour is restricted to the ears and tail only, as in the Turkish Van.

Wedge - Triangular facial conformation seen in most cats except the flat-faced Persian; the shape is elongated in breeds such as the Siamese and Orientals.

Whippy - Of a tail, thin and elastic.

Whisker pads - Fleshy pads on either side of a cat's muzzle where the whiskers are placed in rows.

Wirehair - Rare coat type, caused by a genetic mutation, in which the hairs are twisted or bent at the tips, giving a coarse, springy texture; seen in the American Wirehair cat.

INDEX

INDEX continued

INDEX continued

ACKNOWLEDGMENTS

The publisher would like to thank the following people for their assistance with this book:
For allowing us to photograph their cats: Sphynx and Devon Rex – Susan Rust (ketcherex.tripod.com); Selkirk Rex, Scottish Fold, and British Shorthair – Jan Bradley (www.sheephouse.co.uk); Maine Coon and Ragdoll – Dorothea Uebele (www.applause-pedigreecats.co.uk); Pixiebob and Bengal – Joolz Scarlett (www.arcatia-bengals.com); Siamese and Oriental Shorthair – Pat Cherry (www.ciatra-siamese-orientals.co.uk); Bengal – E A Slater (www.junglefirebengals.co.uk); Persian – Isobella Bangs (lafrebella.tripod.com); American Curl and British Shorthair – Claire Winman (www.americancurls.com).

Tadley Pet Supplies, Baughurst, Hampshire (www.tadleypetsupplies.co.uk), for the loan of cat toys and equipment; Paul Self for equipment photography; Rob Nunn and Myriam Megharbi for additional picture research; Mitun Banerjee for design help; Alison Logan for advice on the "Health and Breeding" chapter; Caroline Hunt for proofreading; and Helen Peters for the index.

The publisher would like to thank the following for their permission to reproduce their photographs:
(Key: a-above; b-below/bottom; c-centre; f-far; l-left; r-right; t-top)

5 Animal Photography: Tetsu Yamazaki (bl). **6-7 Getty Images:** Michelle McMahon / Flickr Open. **9 Alamy Images:** Blickwinkel (br). **Dreamstime.com:** Natalya Sidorova (cl). **10 Dreamstime.com:** Dragonika (cl). **11 Dreamstime.com:** Lrlucik. **12 Dreamstime.com:** Melinda Fawver (bl). **13 Dreamstime.com:** Pjatochka (cl). **14 fotoLibra :** Darran Scott (b). **20 Alamy Images:** Juniors Bildarchiv GmbH (bl). **21 Dreamstime.com:** Marko Bojanovic. **22 Alamy Images:** Juniors Bildarchiv GmbH (b). **23 Alamy Images:** ZUMA Press, Inc. (bl). Dreamstime.com: Jura Vikulin (tr). **24-25 Alamy Images:** Juniors Bildarchiv GmbH. **27 Animal Photography:** Sally Anne Thompson (bl). **29 Alamy Images:** Petographer (ca). Janet Poulsen (b, tr). **31 Larry Johnson:** (cl, b, tr). **37 Dreamstime.com:** Sheila

Bottoms. **40 Ardea:** Jean-Michel Labat (cl, tr); Jean Michel Labat (b). **41 Alamy Images:** Tierfotoagentur (cl, tr, b). **46 Animal Photography:** Alan Robinson (cl, tr, b). **48 Alamy Images:** Top-Pet-Pics. **52 Animal Photography:** Helmi Flick (cl, tr, b). **53 Alamy Images:** Juniors Bildarchiv GmbH (cl, b, tr). **54-55 Dorling Kindersley:** Tracy Morgan- Animal photography. **58 Chanan Photography:** (cl, b, tr). **59 Animal Photography:** Alan Robinson (cl, tr). **61 Animal Photography:** Tetsu Yamazaki (b). **Dreamstime.com:** Vladyslav Starozhylov (cl, tr). **62-63 Alamy Images:** Zoonar GmbH. **65 Fotolia:** Callalloo Candcy (b). **67 Corbis:** Yoshihisa Fujita / MottoPet / amanaimages. **68-69 Dorling Kindersley:** Tracy Morgan-Animal Photography. **72-73 Dreamstime.com:** Lilun. **78 Alamy Images:** Juniors Bildarchiv GmbH (cl); Tierfotoagentur (tr, b). **79 Animal Photography:** Tetsu Yamazaki (cl, tr, b). **81 Alamy Images:** MJ Photography. **82 Petra Mueller:** (cl, bl, br, tr). **84-85 Animal Photography:** Alan Robinson. **86 Animal Photography:** Helmi Flick (cl, tr, b). **87 SuperStock:** Marka (b, cl, c, tr). **88 Getty Images:** Datacraft Co Ltd. **90 Chanan Photography:** (cl, tr). Robert Fox: (b). **91 Animal Photography:** Helmi Flick (cl, tr, c, b). **93 Animal Photography:** Tetsu Yamazaki (cl, tr, b). **Dreamstime.com:** Sarahthexton (c). **96 Alamy Images:** Juniors Bildarchiv GmbH (c, tr, b). **naturepl.com:** Ulrike Schanz (cl). **97 Animal Photography:** Helmi Flick (tr); Tetsu Yamazaki (cl, b). **98 Animal Photography:** Helmi Flick (b, tr). **SuperStock:** Juniors (cl). **99 Animal Photography:** Helmi Flick (b). **Ardea:** Jean-Michel Labat (cl, tr). **100 Getty Images:** Benjamin Torode / Flickr. **101 Dreamstime.com:** Ekaterina Cherkashina (cl, b); Linncurrie (c, tr). **102 Animal Photography:** Helmi Flick (cl, b, tr). **103 Alamy Images:** Idamini (c, tr, b). **104 Animal Photography:** Helmi Flick (c, tr, b). **105 Animal Photography:** Helmi Flick (cl, b, tr). **106-107 Dorling Kindersley:** Tracy Morgan-Animal Photography. **108 Animal Photography:** Helmi Flick (cl, tr, b). **109 Animal Photography:** Tetsu Yamazaki (cl, tr, b). **110 Alamy Images:** Juniors Bildarchiv GmbH (c). **Animal**

Photography: Alan Robinson (cl). **111 Animal Photography:** Helmi Flick (cl, tr, b). **112 Dreamstime.com:** Elena Platonova (tr, b); Nelli Shuyskaya (cl). **113 Animal Photography:** Helmi Flick (cl, b, tr). **114 Animal Photography:** Sally Anne Thompson. **116 Chanan Photography:** (tr, cl, b). **117 Dave Woodward:** (cl, b, tr). **118-119 Dorling Kindersley:** Tracy Morgan-Animal Photography. **120 Fotolia:** Artem Furman (cl, tr, b). **121 Fotolia:** eSchmidt (cl, tr, b). **122 Alamy Images:** Tierfotoagentur (cl, tr, b). **123 Animal Photography:** Alan Robinson (cl, tr, b). **124-125 Dorling Kindersley:** Tracy Morgan-Animal Photography. **126 Dreamstime.com:** Oleg Kozlov. **128-129 Dorling Kindersley:** Tracy Morgan-Animal Photography. **130 Alamy Images:** Juniors Bildarchiv GmbH (tr, b); Tierfotoagentur (cl). **131 Animal Photography:** Tetsu Yamazaki (cl, tr, b). **132 Dorling Kindersley:** Dawn Trick (cl). **135 Dreamstime.com:** Victoria Purdie (bl). **136-137 Dorling Kindersley:** Tracy Morgan-Animal Photography. **138 Chanan Photography:** (b, tr, c). **143 Alamy Images:** Juni.rs Bildarchiv GmbH (b). **Dreamstime.com:** Petr Jilek (cl, tr). **144-145 Alamy Images:** JTB Media Creation, Inc.. **147 Chanan Photography:** (b, cl, tr). **149 Dreamstime.com:** Isselee (cl, tr, b). **151 Chanan Photography:** (b, tr, cl). **153 Alamy Images:** Petra Wegner. **158 Chanan Photography:** (tr, cl, b). **163 Alamy Images:** PhotoAlto. **164-165 Dorling Kindersley:** Tracy Morgan-Animal Photography. **166-167 Corbis:** Julie Habel. **169 Animal Photography:** Tetsu Yamazaki (cl, b, tr). **171 Alamy Images:** Petra Wegner (cl, tr, b). **172 Animal Photography:** Tetsu Yamazaki (cl, tr, b). **173 Dreamstime.com:** Prillfoto (tr). **174-175 Alamy Images:** Juniors Bildarchiv GmbH. **174 Ardea:** Jean-Michel Labat (b). **177 Alamy Images:** Tierfotoagentur (cl, bl, tr). **Animal Photography:** Tetsu Yamazaki (b). **179 Animal Photography:** Tetsu Yamazaki (cl, tr, b). **180 Animal Photography:** Tetsu Yamazaki (cl, b, tr). **181 Animal Photography:** Tetsu Yamazaki (cl, tr, b). **182 Animal Photography:** Helmi Flick (c, tr, b). **184-185 Dorling Kindersley:**

Tracy Morgan-Animal Photography. **186 Alamy Images:** Idamini (tl, tr, b). **187 Alamy Images:** Idamini. **188 Chanan Photography:** (cl, tr, b). **189 Animal Photography:** Helmi Flick (cl, tr, b). **190-191 Dorling Kindersley:** Tracy Morgan-Animal Photography. **193 Animal Photography:** Helmi Flick (tr, b); Tetsu Yamazaki (cl). **194 Animal Photography:** Tetsu Yamazaki (cl, tr, b). **195 Olga Ivanova:** (cl, tr, b). **196 Animal Photography:** Helmi Flick (cl, tr, b). **197 Animal Photography:** Leanne Graham. **198 Alamy Images:** Corbis Premium RF (bl). **199 Dreamstime.com:** Ijansempoi. **200-201 Alamy Images:** Arco Images GmbH. **202 Dreamstime.com:** Joyce Vincent (bl). **203 Alamy Images:** imagebroker (cl). **Corbis:** Michael Kern / Visuals Unlimited (tc). **204 Dreamstime.com:** Stuart Key (tr). **207 Corbis:** Image Source (t). **Dreamstime.com:** Maxym022 (br). **210 Alamy Images:** Juniors Bildarchiv GmbH (l). **212 Photoshot:** NHPA (b). **214 Dreamstime.com:** Saiko3p (t). **215 Alamy Images:** Juniors Bildarchiv GmbH (tr). **216 Dreamstime.com:** Frenc (tr); Eastwest Imaging (l). **217 Alamy Images:** Juniors Bildarchiv GmbH (tl). **218 Dreamstime.com:** Jeroen Van Den Broek (cr). **219 Dreamstime.com:** Niderlander (br). **220 Corbis:** Frank Lukasseck (b). **221 Dreamstime.com:** Mitja Mladkovic. **223 Dreamstime.com:** Mimnr1 (tr). **Fotolia:** Callalloo Candcy. **225 Alamy Images:** Rodger Tamblyn (crb). **226 Dreamstime.com:** Miradrozdowski (cr). **231 Alamy Images:** Juniors Bildarchiv GmbH (cl, tr). **232 Ardea:** John Daniels (bl). **233 Dreamstime.com:** Willeecole (r). **235 Dreamstime.com:** Jana Horová (tl). **236-237 Corbis:** D. Sheldon / F1 Online. **238 Fotolia:** Eléonore H (cr). **239 Getty Images:** Fuse. **240 Fotolia:** Callalloo Candcy (tr). **241 Getty Images:** Danielle Donders - Mothership Photography / Flickr Open (cb). **243 Fotolia:** svetlankahappy (tl). **247 Photoshot:** Juniors Tierbildarchiv

All other images © Dorling Kindersley. For further information see: www.dkimages.com